Published in 2003 by frieze

5-9 Hatton Wall, London ECIN 8HX

Tel +44 (0)20 7813 5555

Fax +44 (0)20 7813 7779

Email editors@frieze.com

www.frieze.com

frieze is an imprint of Durian Publications Ltd., registered in England number 2609458

ISBN 0 9527414 2 3

A catalogue record for this book is available from the British Library

Edited by Emily King

Designed by Christopher Wilson

Consultant Peter Saville

Research by Daniel Mason

Technical consultant Nick Booth

Additional photography by Nick Turner and Dan Fox

Original reprographics by Idea Digital Imaging Ltd.

Additional reprographics by Tag, London

Printed by Butler and Tanner, Frome and London

Distributed outside North and South America
by Thames and Hudson Ltd.

181A High Holborn, London WC1V 7QX

Tel +44 (0)20 7845 5000

Fax +44 (0)20 7845 5050

Email sales@thameshudson.co.uk

www.thameshudson.com

Cover *Unknown Pleasures 2003 (white)* by Bill Holding at Morph UK

Inside covers *Home* and *Brown Eyes, Blue Robe, 3pm* by Sarah Morris 1998

P.1 From a cartoon strip featuring two cowboys that was pasted on the walls of the University
of Strasbourg in 1968. Later it was used by Tony Wilson as the first Factory poster

Title page Martha Ladly and Peter Saville, Paris by Brett Wickens 1982

P.192 After a 1967 interview with Andy Warhol

Contents

Preface

Emily King

This book is the first devoted to the work of Peter Saville. It is arranged in a rough chronology around several essays and an interview and covers everything from Saville's earliest designs for Factory Records to his most recent self-initiated projects. Taking in twenty-five years of Saville's career, the book shows a highly edited selection of output and the result is page after page of popular culture's best known images.

    The title *Designed by Peter Saville* is misleadingly straightforward. Look back through Saville's work and you will see numerous different formulations of credit: 'Sleeve design by Joy Division and Peter Saville'; 'Typographics: Peter Saville'; 'Kelly Saville Associates'; 'Design: Dessin Controlée'; 'Typography: Grafica Industria'; 'Design: B. Wickens & P. Saville for D/R Institut (UK)'; 'Cover by Peter Saville Associates, London'; 'Design Key/PSA'; 'Art direction Peter Saville, designed by Howard Wakefield'. Some of these, particularly the early ones, are achingly self-conscious rebuttals to the conventions of the design industry. Others simply reflect different ways of assigning roles and organising a business. Read in sequence they create a sense of permanent flux that not only mirrors Saville's working mode, but also suggests something more general about the discipline of graphic design. Throughout its short history, graphics has been subject to a series of profound technological and cultural shifts. As a consequence there are almost as many ways of being a graphic designer as there are designers themselves.

    Over the last twenty-five years Saville has explored several different manners of working and various styles of professional presentation, but consistent across time has been his close collaborations with others. As much as possible everyone has been given credit. In cases of omission, please read credit as implied. Instead

Snowdonia 2000
Photography Peter Saville

Studio logotypes 1979–82

of being the last word on Saville and his associates, this book raises the possibility of many other publications. Two spring to mind immediately: a look at the ongoing contribution of Peter's long-term partner Brett Wickens and a proper assessment of the photography of the late Trevor Key. We hope the seeds of these projects are germinating in the following pages. Far from subsuming the work of co-designers and photographers, this book is a celebration of all involved.

Peter Saville would like to thank Trevor Key and Nick Knight, Paul Barnes, Paul Hetherington, Howard Wakefield and Brett Wickens.

He would also like to acknowledge James Adams, Martyn Atkins, Boris Bencic, Anna Blessmann, Paul Brown, Peter Davidson, Michaela Eischeid, Sharon Ellis, Cara Gallardo, Mette Heinz, Angus Hyland, Ken Kennedy, Yvette Lacey, Martha Ladly, Chris Mathan, Fiona McNab, Julian Morey, Gary Mouat, Paul Neale, Helen Noel, Sarah Parris, Phil Pennington, Tim Quay, Victoria Sawdon, Richard Smith, Yvonne Sporre, Paul West, Steven Wolstenholme, Marc Wood and Jon Wozencroft.

Grateful thanks to all clients and collaborators, particularly Tom Attencio, Rebecca Boulton, Rob Gretton, Alan Parks, Lothar Schirmer and Michael Shamberg and those who offered useful information and advice on this publication, including Brett Anderson, Marc Ascoli, Sheridan Coakley, Mark Fenwick, Mark Francis, Malcolm Garrett, Ben Kelly, Mike Meiré, Nicholas Serota and Tony Wilson.

Thanks to all who contributed to the production of the book, particularly Nick Booth and Dan Fox at frieze, Bill Holding at Morph UK, Esther Johnson, Martin Orpen at Idea Digital Imaging, Floyd Palmer at FPD and Nick Turner.

Christopher Wilson would like to thank Phil Baines and Richard Hollis for their useful comments on the book's design.

Special thanks to all at Peter Saville's studio including Sascha Behrendt, Sam Roberts, Tom Skipp and Marcus Werner Hed.

8

Portrait of Peter Saville 2002
Wolfgang Tillmans

When routine bites hard

Emily King

Like the surfer on the cover of New Order's single *Ruined in a Day*, Peter Saville is forever on the crest of something new. He lives in the moment between his life up to that point (a productive but ultimately unsatisfying affair) and his life beyond – a compromised but more lucrative prospect. He inhabits the word-filled gap between parched cliffs and foamy seas. Coming across Saville in his perpetual state of change, legions of journalists have been flattered into believing that they are witnessing a personal revolution. Usually they hang it on an obvious chronological peg – turning thirty, mid-thirties, turning forty and so on – but the truth is it has always been like this and it is unlikely ever to be any different.

Saville's incurable disillusionment, however, is tempered by his insatiable appetites. A lengthy and elaborate tale of weariness, when delivered by someone lounging in a silk dressing-gown on a leather sofa, can be enjoyed with melodramatic relish rather than taken to heart. Mike Meiré, part-time resident of The Apartment (the most Peter Saville of all Saville's dwellings) described the designer's speech as 'as a sculpture of words'; it is a performance that remains compelling, even as it becomes more and more abstract. This brief account of Saville's life was plucked from his colossus of words and backed up by accounts from some of his closest collaborators. Pummelled into a few thousand words it no longer bears much resemblance to Saville's verbal creation, but, read through a veil of smoke with the slack tingle of caffeine in your veins, it might summon up a sense of its shadow.

Saville traces the origins of his distinctive graphic style to a single stolen library book. During his first year of a graphic design course at Manchester Polytechnic, he was joined by his former schoolmate Malcolm Garrett, who had abandoned the

Stanlow 2003
Photography Aidan O'Rourke

Ruined in a Day New Order
London single 1993
Art direction Peter Saville
Design Howard Wakefield
and James Adams at Icon

Le Valium Roche
Catalogue cover 1965
Design Jan Tschichold

My Life in the Bush of Ghosts
David Byrne/Brian Eno
EG album 1981
Video image Brian Eno
Design Peter Saville

typography and graphic communications degree course at Reading University after only one year. Returning to Manchester, Garrett brought with him the fundamentals of a historically rooted design education and the University library's copy of Herbert Spencer's *Pioneers of Modern Typography* (1969). In the late seventies teaching methods at Manchester were stuck in a sixties notion of timeless, contextless graphic communication and Garrett's historical interests were entirely anomalous. Once at Manchester Polytechnic, Garrett combined his long-standing interest in Pop Art, particularly in the silkscreens of Andy Warhol, with his university design education. This gave birth to what Saville describes as 'Day-Glo constructivism' and by his second year at Manchester Polytechnic Garrett was designing startling and original record sleeves for the Buzzcocks. Inspired to raid the treasure chest to similar effect, Saville began to leaf through *Pioneers*.

Amongst the designers included in Spencer's book Saville was most drawn to Herbert Bayer and Jan Tschichold. Rejecting Bayer on the grounds that the work was too close to the ideas that Garrett was exploring, he plumped wholeheartedly for Tschichold. In typographic circles, Tschichold is known for the schism that divides his career. As a young man he pursued hard-line modernist typography, favouring sans serif typefaces and insisting on the asymmetrical setting of type, but later he began to associate these fixed ideas with the ideology of fascism and turned back to serif type and centred settings. Taking on Tschichold's style, Saville didn't distinguish between these two phases, and instead adopted the whole body of work as a singular expression of typographic cool, the opposite to the frantic tussle of contemporary punk typography. This freewheeling approach to design history has attracted some criticism, particularly in the late 1980s when it became fashionable to atone for the style decade, but to censor Saville for his use of the past is to suggest that a slavish following of the historical always trumps a grasp of contemporary codes.

According to Garrett, Saville's concentration on Spencer's book to the exclusion of all else is misleading and typical of Saville's ability to create clean lines from an uncertain tangle, both in anecdote and in design. Garrett remembers many more influences, both historical and contemporary, and endless discussions of possible design routes. Describing his own and Saville's art school selves, he plots a range of alliances, influences and similarities: Garrett thrilled to Hawkwind, whereas Saville was obsessed with Roxy Music; Garrett favoured the messy discursive design of Barney Bubbles, whereas Saville pursued the grand icons in the style of Hipgnosis (a comparison which Saville would acknowledge, but qualify with his own references to fashion set against Hipgnosis' apparent pursuit of the eternal); Garrett was Brian Eno to Saville's Bryan Ferry.

Garrett started working for the Buzzcocks after meeting Howard Devoto and Pete Shelley through the Manchester music scene in 1976. Two years later Saville heard that Tony Wilson, a TV presenter and another Manchester music scene personality was launching new club night and might employ a designer. First approaching Wilson at a Patti Smith gig at the Apollo in January 1978, Saville met him a few months later at the Granada TV canteen. Instead of showing samples of work, Saville let him see pages from Tschichold's *Die Neue Typographie* (1927), and on that basis, he was commissioned to do the first Factory poster. Saville wanted this poster to be the 'coolest, least home-made looking' image possible. Borrowing an industrial warning sign that he had seen on a door at art college, Saville placed it on

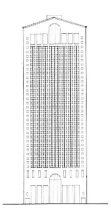

AT&T building, New York
Philip Johnson 1978–84

A Factory Sample Various artists
Factory EP 1978
'Packaged by Peter'
See also p.57

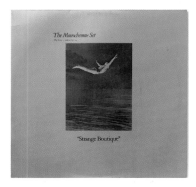

The Strange Boutique The Monochrome Set
DinDisc album 1980
Design Peter Saville

an NCP (National Car Parks) yellow background and framed it with thick rules and sans serif type. Later called Fac 1, this poster was Saville's first classical/modernist combination piece. At the time he was delighted to have done a piece of work that 'didn't look at all like Malcolm's work'.

In July 1978 Saville graduated from Manchester with a first class degree. This honour came courtesy of the external examiner Arnold Schwartzman, a designer who had only seen Saville's work at his final show, the Factory poster amongst other examples. Unlike Saville's tutors, Schwartzman had not experienced Saville's near-constant absence from college, nor been scandalised by his leopard skin and mirror-tiled drawing board (a Roxy-inspired affectation that was vandalised by fellow students). For six months after graduation Saville hung around Manchester, financially supported by his family and doing little other than designing a couple more Factory posters. During this period, while the colour of the general design palette turned Day-Glo, Saville's own tastes veered more toward the classical. On a trip to London, Saville picked up a book describing the architect Philip Johnson's proposals for the AT&T building in New York. To Saville, Johnson's broken pediment in pink stone resonated with his own white Garamond on a black background, and, on the grounds of pure currency, he felt his preferences were endorsed: 'I saw it all as fashion, the mood of the time expressed through design.'

Saville's next major project was the sleeve for *A Factory Sample*. Wilson had been bequeathed a small amount of money by his aunt, and he, Saville and Factory's third founding partner Alan Erasmus decided to release a compilation of tracks by Manchester bands who had yet to secure record contracts. The sampler, which included tracks by Joy Division, The Durutti Column, Cabaret Voltaire and John Dowie, was called Fac 2 according to a numbering system that referenced situationism and the interest in seriality of artists such as John Cage (a system that Wilson continues to employ to this day). Made out of industrial, heat-sealed polythene, the sleeve of Fac 2 was a reworking of the Fac 1 poster in black and silver. Saville remembers the record sounding 'awful', but all the same, the first 5,000 pressings sold out and Factory were left with a small profit and inundated with tapes from other bands looking for representation.

And so Factory Records was born. The first Factory album was Joy Division's *Unknown Pleasures* (1979). Placing an abstract scientific image (chosen by members of the band from the Cambridge Encyclopaedia of Astronomy) in an acutely minimalist setting on luxurious, grained paper, Saville created the look of the definitive new wave album. Listening to the tracks for the first time several weeks after designing the sleeve, Saville was struck with the realisation that 'at that moment everything would change'. On the verge of leaving Manchester for London in the spring of 1979, he realised how fortunate he was to have stayed around for as long as he had.

The first six months after Saville's move to London were unsettled. His work was appreciated, but failed to win him jobs at the major studios, run by design principals who recognised that Saville's talents were not going to be easy to harness for corporate profit. Saville was on the verge of giving up and returning to Manchester when he was given a job by Ian Murray who ran a small design studio called Acrobat. Murray first employed Saville as a studio designer, but later allowed him to go freelance, a concession to his inability to function in the corporate

13

Detail from *1981–1982* New Order
Factory Benelux EP 1982
Painting Martha Ladly

A Basket of Roses Henri Fantin-Latour
Oil on canvas 1890
National Gallery, London
See also p.81

Brett Wickens 1982

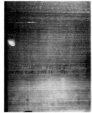

Trevor Key 1987

structure. In spite of Murray's understanding, Saville was more than usually despondent. He found the regular commute between his home in Streatham and the Acrobat studio just off the Edgware Road a strain. It was only in late 1979, when he moved to the Portobello Road offices of DinDisc, an offshoot of Virgin, and took up residence in Holland Park, that Saville's career in London began.

Between 1978 and 1983 Saville created the start-up visual furniture for an entire generation. Forming the spine of the early output are the Joy Division and New Order albums, but these are fleshed out by an improbably large proportion of that era's memorable record sleeves. So many of them that, for anyone born in the mid- to late sixties, looking through the work becomes an unerringly nostalgic experience. The circumstances behind the design of the Joy Division and early New Order sleeves were unique. Members of the band were unable to agree as to what should be on the sleeve and Factory was opposed to putting any kind of constraint on the will of the artist. This left Saville completely free to do as he wished and his response was to create a series of images that were both all about him and all about the client, at the same time. He discovered the mythic middle ground between commercial design and art, a place where the communicative imperative holds, but is unconstrained by the blandness of marketing. The background to Saville's other design was more run of the mill, but all of his output benefited from the central visual experiment.

There is story behind each of Saville's sleeves. Here is a very abbreviated version of one of them:

Looking for an image for the New Order album *Power, Corruption and Lies* (1983) in the postcard racks of London's National Gallery, thinking that he wanted a picture of a Machiavellian despot, Saville came across a flower painting by Henri Fantin-Latour. Apparently not at all suited to the theme, the card prompted the revelation that power is best illustrated by the trappings of wealth. Saville contacted the National Gallery, only to discover that they had no transparency and that the painting was on long loan to Norwich Castle Museum. The next step was to get in touch with the curator at Norwich who, for reasons connected to National Gallery rules and regulations, denied permission to photograph the painting. At this point Wilson became involved. Incensed at the delay, he rang the director of the National Gallery to ask just who it was who owned the painting. The answer came that it was the property of the people of Great Britain, at which point Wilson made the memorable and possibly mythologised declaration: 'The people want it'. The end of the story involves going to Norwich and wrapping a gallery in reams of black velvet to eliminate the reflections from the painting's glass frame, and then discovering that, rather than the grey background of the postcard, the real painting tends toward the brown and having to retint the photograph. But the point of the story is this: whatever Wilson's actual words, he was right. Against the grim background of early Thatcherite Britain, the appropriation of a nineteenth-century still life was a genuinely populist act and the people really, really wanted it.

Saville has been called a 'professional collaborator' and, during his time at DinDisc, he forged some of the most important alliances of his career: those with photographer Trevor Key, with the interior designer Ben Kelly and with Brett Wickens, the holidaying Canadian design student who extended his stay in London by more than ten years. Like wise men bearing gifts, each of them gave Saville

The Haçienda
Ben Kelly Design

Roxy Music *Flesh + Blood*
Polydor poster 1980
Bryan Ferry, Anthony Price, Keil Kirk,
Simon Puxley, Peter Saville

PSA identity 1982

Ken Kennedy
PSA studio, Kensal Road 1983

something he needed. As well as educating him about the ways of the music industry Trevor Key helped Saville tune his photographic eye and leant him his extraordinary image-making capability. Ben Kelly, the designer of the Haçienda, enhanced Saville's sense of materiality and rendered some of his ideas three-dimensional. And Brett Wickens, who became Saville's assistant in 1981 and then a partner in Peter Saville Associates a few years later, had a way with type, and later on with machines, that is key to many of the most Peter Saville-ish of Saville's designs. The other great contributor to Peter Saville-ishness at this time was Bryan Ferry. Designing the covers for two of Roxy Music's most important albums, *Flesh + Blood* (1980) and *Avalon* (1982), Saville spent a lot of time close enough to his idol to see the seams on his suits. By Saville's own admission, he 'studied how to be Bryan first hand'.

After the dissolution of DinDisc in 1982, Saville moved with Key into a studio space on Kensal Road and established Peter Saville Associates (PSA). This era spawned the working practices that remain distinctively Peter Saville: never arriving before lunchtime; working all night at least once a week; always working weekends (often in overcoats because the heating was turned off); and eating dinner at midnight. Alongside Saville and Wickens, various assistants came and went, often reeling away after only a few months, suffering from the physical toll of Saville's unorthodox hours. The Kensal Road period is marked by the crisis of 1985. The ingredients of this crisis were various, including a feeling that historical appropriation had run its course, a broader unhappiness with the idea of graphic design in general (and with the music industry in particular), and a broken heart. Designing the cover for New Order's *Low-life* in 1985, Saville was unable to get his head around postmodern novelty and instead went back to the great standby of music design, portraits of the band members (although the manner in which these portraits were presented is anything but standard). Of course this crisis was not entirely personal. As Saville points out, 1985 was the era of Yohji Yamamoto, Comme des Garçons and all-black minimalism. By moving on from historical reference, Saville remained constant in his pursuit of fashion.

Although Saville stopped the arch business of postmodern appropriation in the mid-1980s, he didn't stop lifting visual motifs for use elsewhere. Referring to the design of the sleeve of *Substance* (1988), which employs a slightly adapted version of Wim Crouwel's 1967 New Alphabet, Saville has said that, by the late eighties, instead of doing 1860, he was doing 1960. As this remark suggests, more than any other graphic designer, Saville is completely honest about the gloriously parasitic element of graphic design.

As well as adding a more modern range of references to his design idiom, Saville also began to flirt with the idea of abstraction. With Key, he invented the dichromat technique, a photographic process analogous to silkscreening, and the details of which remain a secret. Using this method Saville and Key made images of flowers, leaves and eighteenth-century statuary that were used both as New Order sleeves and as independent images. Isolated and radiating unlikely colours, the objects in the dichromat images are reduced to pure aura. Coming closer to the non-representational, and even more involved in unorthodox processes, during the same period Saville was soaking several sheets of metal in a chemical bath. Photographed by Key, the pretty clouds of erosion inspired the industrial metal metaphor on the cover of the 1986 New Order single *State of the Nation*.

15

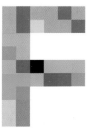

Fruitmarket Gallery
Logo 1985
Design PSA

Lucio Fontana
Whitechapel Art Gallery poster 1988
Design Richard Smith at PSA

World in Motion England New Order
Factory single 1990
Design PSA

Although he was able to apply many of his new ideas to music design, Saville was becoming increasingly weary of the territory. This fatigue coincided with a rising awareness of his work in other areas of the culture industry and in 1985 he was approached by curator Mark Francis to create the identity for the new Fruitmarket Gallery in Edinburgh and in 1986 that for the refurbished Whitechapel Art Gallery (Nicholas Serota's first major project as a museum director). Echoing these white-cubed spaces, Saville's designs were cool and classical. In the case of the Whitechapel, Wickens created a serif typeface with an excavated interior as a metaphor for the gallery's new architecture. Moving closer to the art world, Saville began to think more seriously about being an artist himself. This wasn't a new idea (all non-fine-art art school students have a 'shouldn't I be making art?' moment) but for Saville the issue was not, and still is not, resolved.

Saville's other departure from the music business was into design for fashion, a world introduced to him by the photographer Nick Knight. Saville and Knight first came across one another in the early 1980s when, on the recommendation of graphic designer friends, Knight asked Saville to design a business card. Saville did the job, but made little connection with Knight, who at the time was shaven-headed and specialised in images of skinheads. Three years later, things had changed. After photographing 100 of London's *beau monde* for *i-D* magazine's fifth anniversary issue, Knight was asked by Marc Ascoli to work on the 1986/7 Yohji Yamamoto campaign. He immediately turned to Saville to create a graphic context for his photographs and launched a partnership that survives to this day.

Before being taken on by Yamamoto, Saville went to Paris to meet Ascoli. Knight remembers this encounter as a mutual *coup de foudre*. Arguing that Saville himself could have been a fashion designer, Knight believes that he and Ascoli fell in love with one another's perfectly tuned fashion instincts. The first Yamamoto catalogue by the Ascoli/Knight/Saville team overturned convention by posing models as abstract forms set in pure white space. Saville determined the cropping, sequencing and materiality of this catalogue, creating a document of startling originality. Saville continues to work for fashion, most recently for the designers Alexander McQueen and Stella McCartney. His engagement with fashion's cycle is always ambivalent (he speaks dismissively of 'existentialism one season, polka-dots the next'), but his sensibility is faultless.

In 1988 PSA moved from Kensal Road to Charterhouse Square in East London, an area with a nascent Tribeca feel that Saville found attractive. By this time the company had swollen to ten members, but still had no manager and much of the administration was falling to an overburdened Wickens. Saville remembers feeling frustrated that 'the grown-up things, the business of graphic design wasn't happening', but all the same he took no steps to reorder the company, and instead 'adopted a going for bust attitude, just hoping that something would come along and save the day'. Already in a precarious situation, PSA were completely uninsulated against the world financial crises of 1989 and during the Charterhouse Square period Saville lost all grip on the finances. For several years he had maintained the myth that the company was only around £20,000 in debt, but now was forced to acknowledge that the figure was closer to £100,000. PSA reached an all time low after moving from Charterhouse Square to a temporary space in nearby Ray Street in 1989. For several months it was obvious that the company had to

Automne Hiver 1987–88 Yohji Yamamoto
Art direction Marc Ascoli
Photography Nick Knight
Design Peter Saville

Defilé Printemps Eté 1992 Yohji Yamamoto
Art direction Peter Saville
Photography Trevor Key

Republic New Order
Photoshop test 1993
Image manipulation Brett Wickens

Sunset Strip from the Chateau Marmont
Polaroid Peter Saville 1995

disband and Wickens likens the experience to watching 'an animal in the death throes'. In particular he remembers designing *World in Motion*, New Order's 1990 World Cup single, when things were at their very worst, the hexagonal outlines becoming the template of pure misery.

Through a perverse twist of fate, concurrent with the demise of PSA, Peter Saville's cultural capital reached an all time high. Walking down Oxford Street, Saville saw the influence of his work all around, applied to the fascias of retail outlets by the younger members of large design consultancies, New Order fans every one. In response, Wickens marshalled the help of management consultant Richard Thomas and put together *From Cult To Corporate*, a document outlining how PSA could apply their thinking to the mainstream and cash in on their own cultural achievement. Looking back, Saville feels this document was a mistake. At the time he believed that corporations would want to buy cult cool; now he knows that they merely want to copy. But while the idea of selling out might have been misconceived, the document did encourage others to buy in. Wickens and Saville circulated it around a number of London's larger design firms and attracted some interest. While still considering offers, in 1990 Saville was invited by John McConnell to become a partner at Pentagram.

Joining Pentagram involved taking on a system that had been in place since the company was founded in 1972. Saville became the head of a team made up of Wickens and the bulk of the PSA studio and assigned an earning target of twice his previous studio turnover. His Pentagram salary gave him the leverage to avoid the ignominy of bankruptcy by the narrowest of margins. Interviewed by Rick Poynor at around this time, Saville spoke of the Pentagram ways, timesheets and the like, 'with the zeal of the newly converted'. Unsurprisingly this didn't last. In spite of hiking up his day rate, in his two-year trial period Saville's team never pulled in more than £250,000 a year. At the international partners' meeting held in Jamaica in December 1992, he remembers feeling a cool wind amongst the tropical breezes.

Saville's time at Pentagram is summed up by a single image, that of six men around a Mac. The team was designing the sleeve of New Order's *Republic*. Saville had the idea of juxtaposing dissonant stock photographs and Wickens had just achieved the perfect Photoshop blend. Howard Wakefield, who joined Saville's team as Wickens' assistant, recalls huge excitement, each of them taking turns to 'drive the Mac'. Amongst the six men this was something of a eureka moment, but from the outside it appeared no more than a huge waste of money. On seeing the cluster McConnell is said to have imagined the combined hourly rate and remarked 'that looks expensive'. According to Wickens the proximity of partner and computer in itself was enough to arouse suspicion. While Wickens had become increasingly involved in technology since PSA bought their first Mac in 1987, he describes a general hostility toward computers at Pentagram, stemming from the belief that keyboards were the tools of technicians.

Wickens and Saville began contemplating their next move well before they were asked to leave Pentagram on the conclusion of Saville's probationary period in February 1993. In the summer of 1992 they had travelled to Los Angeles to design an identity for an educational television channel and, residing for a month at the Sunset Marquis hotel, had been seduced by the city. Once it became obvious Saville's partnership was at an end, they began seeking a means to return. Led by Wickens'

17

Rustic Canyon 1993
After John Kacere
Art direction Peter Saville
Photography Klaus Laubmayer

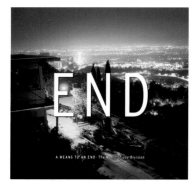

A Means to an End Various artists
Hut album 1995
Art direction Peter Saville
Photograph Dean Chamberlayne
Design Howard Wakefield

Universal Family
Proposal on the theme of evolution
for Mandarina Duck 1995
Photography Mitchell Funk

interest in multimedia, they envisioned a marriage of the movie industry and the new technology, and proposed the idea to Aubrey Balkind of New York-based design firm Frankfurt Balkind. At the time Frankfurt Balkind had an LA outpost that was involved in Hollywood promotion; by shipping Saville and Wickens out to LA, Balkind hoped to create and dominate new areas of movie-related design.

It didn't work out like that. Saville's commitment to the scheme was minimal and the shameless commercialism of Hollywood was antithetical to his way of working. Neither drumming up new business, nor doing the design jobs that had been found for him at Frankfurt Balkind, Saville spent his first few months in LA shopping. His clothes and furniture had been impounded by US customs and, using Frankfurt Balkind's credit card, he applied himself to buying replacements worthy of a Hollywood lifestyle. Wickens meanwhile continued to believe in the convergence of technology and 'infotainment'. Hoping to create some kind of future on the West Coast, he began to distance himself from Saville.

In December 1993, Balkind took away the overstretched credit card and started giving Saville a small weekly cash allowance. From then on Saville's LA experience careered downhill. In spite of living in a now well-furnished Hollywood Hills house with panoramic views, each day he struggled to find cash for food and petrol. No longer welcome at the Frankfurt Balkind studio, Saville began to operate from Swingers Diner on Beverley Boulevard. Enrolling the 17 January 1994 earthquake into his tale of woe, Saville recalls experiencing the aftermath of the disaster with only $3 in his pocket. Amongst the more romantic of personal nadirs, this period is expressed beautifully by Dean Chamberlayne's photograph of the view from Saville's house juxtaposed with the single word 'End', a piece designed for a Joy Division covers album. By the time Saville left LA in the summer of 1994, Wickens had established himself with Frankfurt Balkind, where he worked until 1998, and their thirteen-year partnership came to a close.

On his return to London, Saville was surprised to find how much the city had changed. He had missed the dawn of Brit-art and Brit-pop, and now encountered both of them at their most expansive. There was a feeling that 'the stakes had changed'. At first Saville found this disorienting, but after a few months he was reabsorbed into the over-excited, mid-nineties mêlée. Reunited with his former assistant Howard Wakefield, late in 1994 he was asked to design the sleeve for *(The Best of) New Order* and early in 1995 he was asked to review the Mandarina Duck identity, a job worthy of a full Pentagram rate. Around the same time Saville and Wakefield were offered space at Tomato, the design firm at the swirling core of Brit hysteria. Although neither Saville nor Wakefield felt at home at Tomato, and left after only six months to lead a nomadic life amongst Soho's temporary work spaces, the invitation confirmed Saville's place in London's new hierarchy.

1995 was a good year for Saville: outgoings were relatively low and income was steady. All the same he was very unsettled, living with friends and working at hired desks. In his search for a place to live, Saville had been shown an apartment that was as near as possible his natural habitat, a run-down Mayfair pad decorated in seventies coke-dealer style. At the time he was unable to afford the rent, but a few months later he met Mike Meiré, the co-founder of a young German advertising agency Meiré and Meiré (and a grown-up New Order fan), who was looking for a London base. Between them Meiré and Saville planned a glamorous live/work

the apartment 1995
Photograph Henry Bourne

This is Hardcore Pulp
Island single 1998
Art direction John Currin and Peter Saville
Photography Horst Diekgerdes
Design Howard Wakefield
and Paul Hetherington

GIVENCHY

Identity 2002
Art direction Peter Saville
Typographic consultant Paul Barnes

space, an apartment that would perfectly express Peter Saville and also provide a London base for Meiré and Meiré. Meiré signed a three-year lease on 10 Audley Court and Saville invited his long-term colleague Ben Kelly to refurbish.

The results were glorious and soon after moving in early in 1996 every lifestyle magazine in London had been in touch. Saville's suede bedroom walls, long leather sofa and Verner Panton shell chandelier were the apotheosis of the languidly vulgar luxury that was to become fashionable. Following the style press, a new generation of music clients arrived. Bands like Pulp and Suede had seen the pictures of the apartment and were attracted to the image. Through Meiré, who was an art collector and a friend of gallerist Jay Jopling, a number of young artists also paid visits and these encounters reawakened Saville's interest in producing art. During this period Saville's work was a direct expression of where and how he was living. The whole Peter Saville 'thing' was beginning to cohere – he was inhabiting every part of his myth.

Although life and work were all coming together, the financial aspects of the arrangement were less well resolved. During his time at 10 Audley Court Saville worked under the name The Apartment and was paid a salary by Meiré and Meiré, which gave him the freedom to linger on each piece of work. In particular Meiré remembers Saville dwelling on the Suede sleeves for several weeks, as if the screen were a canvas. This was very productive in terms of Saville's work, but less so in terms of the return on Meiré and Meiré's outlay. After two and a half years Meiré realised that his company could not sustain the arrangement and, regretfully he pulled out, taking his only London staff member Michaela Eischeid with him. Saville lived out the last six months of the lease, working with Wakefield and Paul Hetherington. Having recently discovered the latest properties of Photoshop, the three of them spent hours recycling images into seductive abstract arrangements that Saville calls Waste Paintings.

At the end of the nineties, the height of the dot.com frenzy, Saville's attention was drawn to the web. Realising that the internet allowed the individual to distribute work without the intervention of any other agent, Saville thought that this medium might offer a platform for his client-free ventures. Saville's long-time collaborator Nick Knight was thinking along similar lines and between them they imagined a website that would be first a forum for new work and later a digital gallery. For a long time Knight had been aware that Saville was dissatisfied with the business of graphic design ('He is the best at what he does, but he doesn't think that's enough') and he hoped the internet might create an escape route. Excited by the prospect of a new direction for himself and Saville, Knight was prepared to invest in this idea and, a few months after the lease of 10 Audley Court came to an end, he rented a space on St John Street as a live/work space for Saville and a base for their internet experiment. Knight and Saville called their site Show (after a suggestion by artist Sarah Morris), and after a long time in development, it took to the web early in 2001 at the address showstudio.com.

Like many of its internet contemporaries, the purpose of SHOWstudio was never entirely clear. There had been ideas of profit, but soon after its launch it had become obvious that the internet was more money pit than gold mine. Knight moved the SHOWstudio team from St John Street to Ironmonger Row and Saville moved with them, but beyond contributing the odd project to what remains

19

Factory Communications
Logos 1980 and 1990
Art direction Peter Saville
Factis90 typeface by Brett Wickens
Redrawn after Rotis by Otl Aicher

Factory®

amongst the most stylish sites around, he had less and less to do with the project. In summer 2002 Saville moved upstairs from SHOWstudio and since then he has been working with a fluid team of independent designers and creative consultants. Saville's client list now includes Stella McCartney and Givenchy and his achievement lies in being able to suggest that these companies have existed forever at the same time as placing them precisely in fashion's endless now.

As well as this commercial work Saville continues to develop independent design ideas, ideas akin to those he applied to the sleeves of New Order, but now without a client. He misses the old days of Factory, when he was employed by a client who had an instinct for culture (not commerce) and allowed him to communicate beyond the market to the great wide world. In overly modest moments, Saville credits his success entirely to the extraordinary circumstances of his early career. For someone who grew up designing New Order sleeves, the business of interpreting the client's message can seem very tame. Saville doesn't just want to change the message, he wants to tamper with the commercial and cultural frameworks that gave rise to such a message in the first place.

Saville's story can be read as a refusal of commercial success. The moments he has come closest to being able to carve up his talent for considerable profit are those when he has behaved as his very worst. Although this could be seen as a high-minded stand against prostituting his skill, it is nothing of the sort. Saville would sell out if he could, but he is constitutionally unable. He may once have spoken enthusiastically about timesheets, but that was pure fantasy. The idea of putting x days into a job that paid £y is incompatible with his way of working. At Saville's studio everything is done afresh and everything takes the time it needs, which can be enough days to make a client sweat, but when was getting something just right the work of an instant? Some of Saville's former clients suggest that his output is unnaturally truncated, that he has failed to do all the work he should. This isn't true. Instead Saville has been engaged on a lifelong process of self-editing. The selection of images shown in this book are the greatest hits of a career that is composed of almost nothing but.

At PSA studio, Kensal Road
Photography Tony Barratt 1984

Interview with Peter Saville

Christopher Wilson

You've cited Roxy Music as a prime early influence – you once said, 'from hairdressing to fine art all points were covered'.[1] Was this more of a stance than a philosophy, or did they have something profound to tell you about art and design?

Peter Saville

The Roxy Music influence was during a very formative period for me, between 1973 at the age of eighteen, up until punk in '76. There was a synthesis of influences within the Roxy project that appealed to the visually-orientated of my generation. I was fascinated by the fusion of retro and techno influences that got spun together in Roxy Music. They were the first postmodern experiment in pop. They make sense in the context of everything that came before, in the same way that postmodernism does.

I'd witnessed my older brothers enjoying what the sixties had to offer, and suddenly I'm fifteen, I'm just about to engage with pop culture myself, and it's all over. The dungarees, the hair and the afghans were all terribly bedraggled by 1970. The ones who were still alive had gone to the countryside to recuperate – Paul McCartney was singing *Mull of Kintyre*. And if you were fifteen, just waiting to go to the party, this earthy rehab was really boring. Sex came back in with glam. I found a sexy style-zone through the Roxy covers and the pages of *Club International*, *Men Only* and the fashion magazines. There was a club in Manchester which played exclusively Roxy Music and David Bowie. I was there four nights a week, dressed as Bryan Ferry in a white tuxedo. I would spend all night in this synthetic palace – an entirely self-contained world of retro style fantasy.

The only art movement I knew anything about as a teenager was pop. I saw Roxy Music as a Pop Art concept. They *were* a band, and there was a sound, but I saw the *image* as an art concept rather than a dressing-up. Marc Bolan and David Bowie made an interesting foray into challenging sexual stereotypes, but in the fancy dress

Sundown W12 2002
Photography Peter Saville

Air Hockey 1974
Drawing Peter Saville

Art 1975
Collage Peter Saville

Roxy Music Roxy Music
EG twelve inch album 1972
Concept Bryan Ferry
Art direction Nicholas de Ville
Photography Karl Stoecker
Model Kari-Ann

department, whereas early Roxy synthesised some really quite sophisticated facets of popular culture, from Pop Art to Hollywood. They went back into pre-sixties imagery and ideals, mixed them all up with electronic music, and brought the whole thing back in a modern way. In that respect their iconography was at odds with the clichéd sixties iconography that a young teenager in Manchester knew about.

Did you perceive their mixing of past influences as a matter of parody or tribute?
I thought of it as a kind of love affair – 'Don't we still quite like this?' For example, 'Ladytron' has a synthesiser line with a saxophone over the top, yet boys' own sixties rock didn't have saxophones like that. I was particularly obsessive around the time of Bryan's *These Foolish Things* retro covers album – the sort of thing that somebody a few years older than me absolutely abhorred. It was contradictory to all their values. Here's someone singing a Drifters song – how could anybody be interested in that? But to my generation it was new and different.

There's one other big thing, which has less to do with the music. I saw the Roxy covers as an exercise in communication through styling. They're not about literally what's on them; it's the subtext that they open up and the place where they put the music. It's not really about this picture; it's about what this picture represents, and the context it triggers. It's no surprise that Bryan was taught by Richard Hamilton at Newcastle – the covers are post-Hamilton, post-pop artworks. They're an exercise in their own right, independent of the music.

What did the covers say to you specifically?
They represented what I wanted. Many seventies covers had been mythical: five-year-olds clambering over a multicoloured Giant's Causeway [Led Zeppelin's *Houses of the Holy*, 1973] is just pseudo-mythology, whereas a Roxy cover proposed an idealised – but achievable – vision of the world. Girls can look like that. You can stand by that swimming pool with some chi-chi people lounging in the background. We have a magazine full of it now, called *Wallpaper*. The world that Bryan and Antony Price envisioned now exists. Five-year-olds are not clambering over Giant's Causeway, and blobby Yes logos are not floating in the desert outside Guatemala City. Roxy inspired a generation of creatives to make it happen. I became interested in fashion through the medium of Roxy covers. They charted phase one; my role was to move on to phase two.

You weren't from a working-class background, but was it important that Ferry was?
Bryan was the quintessential middle-class role-model. As an eighteen-year-old it was difficult to look at Sean Connery's James Bond and figure out how you were going to do it, because you're not in a casino and you're not going home in an Aston Martin. But Bryan was a kind of bridge: it could be done within the terms of an existence that you could have. You'd walk through Manchester School of Art in 1974, and all of the groovy, ambitious young men were plainly showing traces of his influence. He was the complete blueprint of and first study course in style culture. 'You can have it if you want it.'

Airport with Julie 1977
Photography Peter Saville

Oh Yeah Roxy Music
Polydor single 1980
Design Peter Saville

You too can walk down Savile Row with Kari-Ann on your arm.
Of course. And that's what I did. I would spend my evenings in that club in Manchester with girls in satin skirts split to the thigh, fishnet stockings, high heels and too much eye makeup. And it was *so* sexy. Especially compared to the …

… dungaree-clad hippies?
Yeah, that my older brother had ended up with. In a field.

In their knowing mixture of retro and brand-new, are Roxy a precursor to Peter Saville?
They're my art college. I learned more from Roxy Music than I did from college. I hadn't thought of it before, but it's true.

Can you see their influence in, for instance, *Power, Corruption and Lies*?
Yes. The influence is in the totality of the image; the creating of an environment in which to place – in this instance – a piece of music. I'd be fine with a Roxy album inside that cover.

But like many of your works, it employs more understated imagery than Roxy's usual fare.
In that sense I'd moved on from glam. My disappointment in that universe was that it didn't evolve. Some of the styling got better and a little more subtle, but for Bryan the albums had to stay literal and figurative. They became a cliché. My own first Roxy single cover is an abstract: the white leather of *Oh Yeah*. 'Is it a wedding chapel bible or the seats of a Corvette?' It's a step forward. We don't need to see a girl driving the car; our reading of semiotics is more refined now.

Roxy fit your idea that visual culture could communicate in a subtle way, rather than by the outright statements of the 'Big Ideas' world – indeed you detested the Big Ideas approach to graphics.
Yes – they weren't Big Ideas anymore. A visual pun is a tiny idea. If you're dealing with something richer, trying to embody it in a pun is myopic and devaluing.

Given that the Big Ideas approach was prevalent when you began, what made you want to be a graphic designer? Did you assume you'd have to toe the Big – or as you say, Little Ideas line?
I didn't know about that yet. When we were in the sixth form at school, Keith Breeden, Malcolm Garrett and I lived in the art room, recreating in watercolour (*laughs*) the pop environment that we identified with. Keith did fantastic versions of Peter Phillips, Malcolm did variations on record covers that he loved – he was particularly good at Hawkwind's *Xin Search of Space* – and I would make gouache versions of custom cars and Alan Aldridge's *The Butterfly Ball* – the first British masterpiece of airbrush.

We had a progressive young teacher called Peter Hancock, who said 'You boys should consider graphic design'. We liked making this kind of imagery, and he told us that there was a profession in it. We decided there and then that we wanted to

The Art Room, St Ambrose College 1972
From left: Keith Breeden, Henrik Lach, Malcolm Garrett, Phillip Norris, Peter Mullens and Peter Saville
Photography Peter Hancock

Bound (detail) Terry Pastor
Airbrush illustration for *Men Only* 1979–80
Based on a previous Pastor work from 1973

How I Feel About Typography 1975
Airbrush illustration Peter Saville

Julie with Sandy 1977
Photography Peter Saville

be graphic designers. We didn't know what it was, but we wanted to be it. It's remarkable how naïve you are at fifteen. But it seemed great, because English, history and geography were getting really like work. This was fun. My academic work was nonexistent for the next two years. I didn't even fill out my English paper.

You sat an exam and didn't do anything?
Yeah. I wrote my name and that was it.

What a premonition.
(*Laughs*) I made stylised, image-based graphics through foundation, but in the first year of the degree course I came up against the recognised formula of graphic design in 1975. It wasn't what I liked. To my dismay, the tutors didn't appreciate the sexy edge of graphic design – the edge which was being influenced by retro style culture and aspects of fine art. My graphic heroes were Bush Hollyhead, Dan Fern and George Hardie, and Terry Pastor, an amazing airbrush illustrator who made sexually deviant imagery influenced by Allen Jones and the fetish world. I discovered Helmut Newton and Guy Bourdin, and was in love with French and Italian *Vogue*. This was the world I was living in in my head, and it was a terrible shock that the graphics staff didn't get it. It probably seemed superficial; they had no value system to judge it by. And of course I went in late, didn't work very hard, and did what I wanted, so we were constantly at odds anyway.

What form did their 'recognised formula' take?
They were trying to teach graphics as epitomised by the recognised practitioners of the time – a Milton Glaser or a Pentagram. But they'd lost their grasp of the moment. The agenda was how to find witty visual puns to summarise a situation: a logo for a restaurant could be a bite out of a plate. Well, to a young person growing up on Roxy Music, that was utterly banal. I won't spend five minutes thinking down that line. It's stupid. It tells me nothing about the restaurant.

What I learned from style culture was if you dress in a particular way, you communicate with other like-minded people. I just employed exactly the same technique with graphics. So forget the bite out of the plate. The choice of type alone will tell you what kind of restaurant this is. Get the typeface, size, position, spacing and mood right, and it will tell you. Is it Le Gavroche or is it McDonald's? It's the language of semiotics, not of puns.

I decided that I had to trust my own instinct, and just do what I felt certain to be right and directional. So sometime during the second year when I saw a book called *Pioneers of Modern Typography* on Malcolm's desk, I thought 'Wow. It's all here.' My academic education began at that point.

When you saw Jan Tschichold's work, did it feel familiar?
It just looked like the graphic formula for the times. It was self-evident that this was how graphics should be now. I was astonished it was all so old – design had been to all these places and had seemingly forgotten or never embraced them. It's the same situation as Roxy: 'Hey, here's a synthesiser and a saxophone. Have you ever heard one of those before? No? Well, the previous era threw it out.' So for me, *Pioneers of Modern Typography* is a pencil skirt.

Die Neue Typographie Jan Tschichold
Publicity leaflet 1928

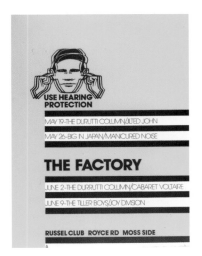

The Factory
Poster 1978
Design Peter Saville
See also p.53

Closer Raf Simons 2003

As opposed to the dungarees?

(*Laughs*) Exactly. I immediately began to integrate this look into my work. Roxy was my BA; my MA started the day I picked up *Pioneers* from Malcolm's desk. And it didn't stop until 1990. It was absolutely full-on, consuming every thing I could from history – where it all came from, what it was all about, and how it crossed over to art and photography and painting and sculpture. I searched high and low for information.

Was it important to you to understand the social context in which such work had come about?

I tried to learn a little. I was good at superficially understanding things, but didn't read enough. I was dilettante-ish. I thought I could decode it from the surface, but some things I didn't decode successfully.

You've often questioned whether graphic design was the appropriate career choice for you. Were there any such doubts during your college days?

I'd had this preconceived idea that I was going to do graphics, because I was so good at creating a graphic façade. But I should have been either a photographer or a fashion designer. My degree show was fifty per cent photography. If I'd thought of it, I could have become a fashion photographer.

But surely it's because you have a fashion designer's sensibility applied in the wrong place that your work has been influential?

Yes, and it's made me a quirky, distinctive graphic designer, but not a professionally successful one. I would have been a more successful menswear designer, because my prime motivation would have been direct to product: I'd be making what I wanted. My first concern each day is what I'm going to wear. How do I feel? What is my identity? I've always had to wait for the manufacturers to get around to things that I knew would happen. I was looking for neo-Gucci long before Tom Ford was able to push it through in the mid-nineties.

So you still regret having had to filter yourself through a surrogate medium?

Fashion might have been too directly satisfying, and the enigmatic qualities that have gone into some of the work probably wouldn't have happened. It's exactly what you're saying: I've had to try to express feelings through a default medium. My covers were fashion statements. *Power, Corruption and Lies* is a neo-sixties floral techno collection; *Low-life* is an existential black polo-neck collection. As cardboard and ink, my collections were enigmas. On a runway they would have looked quite self-evident.

Aren't enigmas much more Saville than 'self-evident' anyway?

Yes, so it's difficult to suppose to what level fashion would have satisfied me. I'm successful by artistic terms, but not at all by professional ones. If you gave me a choice between Wally Olins and Tom Ford, let me be Tom Ford any day. It's one of the dilemmas that I've hit since Pentagram: I didn't want to be in the corporate communications industry. It's boring and unsexy.

27

Fractured Music
Logotype 1980
Typography Martyn Atkins

Rachel 1985
Photography Trevor Key

Which aspects of your fashion sensibility have transposed best to graphic design?
I'm not passionately interested in the construction of a piece of clothing. My understanding of fashion is in the sense of zeitgeist. The thing that fascinates me, which I'm entranced by and psychologically addicted to, is how the arts represent the mood of the moment. In all forms of art and design, from painting to clothes to products to cars to architecture. That's the context I've always seen everything in, even as a teenager. How do the arts manifest the direction of society? How do they represent and influence that mood?

At college I spent very little time in the graphics department, because graphics is not an end in itself. Graphics is the interface, the label. Where are there some ideas, something real to respond to? I'd spend a lot of time with the photographers and fashion designers to see what they were doing. In the refectory I always sat with the groovier people, usually from product design and furniture, and the girls who did fashion and fabrics. That's where I wanted to belong, because (*pauses*) I wanted to be cool. How I had the good fortune to grow up gave me only one ambition in life, and that was to be groovy.

Why?
I suppose I thought it was sexy and attractive, and a good way to get girls. The thing I worried about was that I didn't want to be a geek. I wanted to be good looking, and attractive, and that people would like me. The thing that I was most fascinated by was coolness. Many teenagers are, but it usually passes.

Inherent in the idea of cool is a certain propensity for disloyalty: if what's cool today is not relevant tomorrow, it's thrown out.
That is the worst side of it, and is to some extent how the fashion business works. I can't quite go that far – my superficiality is not as deep as that (*laughs*). I'm more interested in the natural evolution of cool as an ever-expanding overview: cool as a moving target that you have to follow.

To many of those outside of fashion, what you're describing as 'evolution' is merely change: 'We can't do that this season because we did it last season'.
But they're the ones who don't understand it – they sit on the bus and see where it takes them. Actually, that must be great, because it's horrible to always be wondering 'Which turn do we make next?'

Did you immediately know what you wanted in place of visual puns?
Malcolm Garrett and I shared a vision of the world: why couldn't the everyday look better? We might not be able to influence the products themselves, but surely the interface with those products could look better. We were keen to get an opportunity to make something real, something which would exist in our world, instead of working 'virtually' in layout pads on synthetic college problems. And we would do it within the context of our taste at that time.

What formed your interest in mixing classical forms with modern ones?
My mother's home is full of *objets d'art* – paintings, ceramics, glassware – typical aspirational, middle-class antiques. Much of it is clichéd, but some of what appeals to my mother in it is appealing to me. Whether I intellectually agree with it or not,

At PSA studio, Charterhouse Square
Photography Nigel Parry 1988

Cherub 1988
Dichromat Trevor Key and Peter Saville

Run 2 **New Order**
Factory single 1989
Design PSA after Bold

Blue Monday 1995 **New Order**
London single
Art direction Peter Saville
Design Howard Wakefield
See also p.142

there's a coffee-table sensibility in the home, and a lot of that is obviously ingrained in me, because it goes into how I appreciate things, and consequently how I make things. A lot of the time I was doing my damnedest to get away from it. I have sat in my mother's drawing room and looked at these *objets* that I grew up with, and I know how much they influenced me, although I wasn't aware of it. But I also like the new. I used to be quite content to leave the newsstand with an *i-D* and a *Country Life*, because I found interesting points between those two places.

On a trip to London in the early seventies, I bought a packet of soap flakes from the Biba shop – they were packaged in art deco dark brown and beige. I thought 'Why don't supermarkets sell groovy-looking soap flakes?' It was about positioning the product in the context of lifestyle. The first opportunities that came to us were a Buzzcocks cover for Malcolm, and a clothes shop for me.

Of all the badly designed products you saw around you, surely many of them – such as soap flakes – looked generally worse than the average record cover?
Yes, they did. But you don't get much work to do when you're young, because you haven't learned how to do it yet. You certainly aren't given the soap flakes. You're given simple, disposable things to design for other young people.

Would you have preferred the soap flakes commission?
Confronted with the reality, it would be awful. It would be fun to design them the way that Biba had, and to a certain extent Malcolm did that with the first Buzzcocks album – its own silver carrier bag with the word 'Product' on it. The Biba soap flakes were a pre-punk moment. Once punk happened, the aesthetic went through a radical shift.

Getting to do a record cover was fantastic, but pre-'76 it was as far-off an idea as the soap flakes, because the early seventies was an era of supergroups and big business. You were at college in a provincial city. When you went to see a group, you sat with 2,000 others in a large auditorium. It was an entirely removed experience.

In '76 young people requisitioned the leading edge. I remember being at the Electric Circus one night, thinking 'This is what rock'n'roll must have been like twenty years ago'. None of this watching-from-a-hundred-yards-away; it was right there in front of you. It hurt your ears. And then the people who had been making this music were there standing next to you at the bar. And another night someone you'd been talking to was now on stage!

Did your work have an anarchic agenda?
Peter Saville was from the other side of the tracks. My 'anarchic' was totally different to any anarchic self-expression coming from an Ian Curtis or a Peter Hook. My anarchy was in the visual order of things. I didn't have more serious issues to worry about. I was just being a sort of anarchist among the *objets d'art*.

In omitting names and titles, were you trying to make the work more synonymous with art?
It was a pursuit of cool. The people I produced the work on behalf of didn't have any strong feelings about ego or presenting themselves, and agreed with me that it was cooler not to. 'Here's a record. If you like it, you'll find it. I really don't need to tell you any more, do I?' It was an understated detachment, and you get a remarkable

International New Order
London album 2002
Preliminary and final designs
Art direction Peter Saville
Illustration Victoria Sawdon
Design Saville Associates

Music from the edge of Heaven Wham!
Columbia album and logotype 1986
Design PSA

sense of wellbeing from knowing without being told. You can find it yourself, and know it when you've found it. But usually I just couldn't work out how to do the typography. It even happened this week, with *International*. It had a great bit of type, but it kept looking like a record cover, so I took it off.

'It kept looking like a record cover'. What do you want it to look like?
A thing.

Doesn't a record cover constitute a 'thing'?
No, it's a record cover first, and a thing second. I like the idea of it being a thing first and only secondarily a cover.
In his article about *Technique* in *The New York Times*, Jon Pareles referred to the 'mass-produced secret'.[3] The people who wanted that record wanted it because it wasn't blatantly and publicly selling itself. There's an exclusiveness.

It's an odd 'exclusiveness' which can accommodate the fact that *Blue Monday* became the world's biggest-selling twelve-inch single.
But that is the great insult of business: the disrespect to its audience, and the use of the word 'punter'. I've never produced a piece of work for a 'punter'. I'd find it degrading.

How have you gone about retaining that respect when communicating a more mass-market product such as Wham!?
This is the irony: when you produce things for 'punters', even if they're successful, they're not *sustainable*. George Michael made the music that George Michael loved. He just happened to be archetypal of millions. I went to meet him at Basing Street Studio off Portobello, and I can hear the playback of *Wake Me Up Before You Go-Go*, which as a pop song is massive. This twenty-year-old, who I thought was a performer, tells me that he's written, arranged and produced it. I thought 'This guy is fantastic. It may be populist, but it's brilliant. And I can't be snobbish and avant-garde in front of that.'
But there are many jobs where the values I'm trying to present are not the values of the client, and the relationship doesn't work. It's one of the reasons that I'm not doing lots of business, because there are very few situations where there's a genuine sense of belief in what one is doing. The clients realise that there is not a like soul across the table, and it worries them.

Your work has often relied heavily on appropriation. Did you intend this to be especially pertinent to the times?
My generation can only see things in the context of other things that have already happened. So programmed are we by postmodern sensibility – or maybe just the end of belief – that we understand everything referentially. I see this particularly in my creative contemporaries. Everything is like something else: 'It's like Elvis, on speed. It's kind of medieval, in space.' Everything is contextualised and defined retrospectively. If you said 'it's like nothing you've ever seen before', we'd be a bit lost. One of the quintessential pop-culture landmarks of this is *Bonnie and Clyde*, from 1967. It's a retro movie. Warren Beatty has short hair and wears a tweed suit, and suddenly everybody's in love with it: 'Where have the long hair and flares gone?' Stylistically, we quantify things referentially. That's how we understand things now.

Suede *Trash, Saturday night and Lazy*
Nude singles and postcard 1996
Nick Knight, Peter Saville and Brett Anderson
Paintbox Steve Seal
Design Howard Wakefield at the apartment

Were you aware of this at the time?
No. I can see in retrospect how it works. Our culture now relies a lot on familiarity, and this how my work has appealed to people.

If you look at the cultural path of the twentieth century, its aesthetic makes sense up to and including the sixties. There are huge events, but you can see a clear evolution of thinking, speeded by technology. In the late sixties, the unrelenting march stops and has a hangover. Everybody is questioning the ride, and some of the results of it – such as living on the twentieth floor of a housing block. 'Did the baby go out with the bathwater? Has the human experience lost something along the way here? Shouldn't we be restoring and reinventing old buildings instead of knocking them down and building new ones? What have we abandoned, and can we bring it back and look at it again? Maybe some of it was good.' So the early seventies is the period of retrospection and retrievalism.

You're saying that your work's appeal lies in its familiarity, but would 'displaced familiarity' be a more accurate term? We may be familiar with classicism from inscriptions and wine labels, but the effect of it when applied to *Closer* was new and unsettling.
What you've touched upon there is a really good way to understand the whole essence of my approach to communications design. If I have brought *anything* to graphics as a discipline, it's a subtler understanding of semiotics. You referred to inscriptions and wine labels, as codes. The part I played was to utilise those codes in other places. It's a shift of context, and with it come the values of where that code was founded. I was saying that there are some of the qualities or spirit of where *this* originated, in *this* new product.

If you listen to *Closer*, you tap in to some timeless values and feelings. Those values of a deeply-rooted classicism are exuded by that choice of typeface and that antique paper. You can read it there between the lines.

Your referentialism seems to rely on the idea that the original referent must be from some other culture outside of – in this case – pop music.
Absolutely. We weren't engaged with any pop references at that point. What you see now is a new and sometimes intelligent referentialism within pop itself.

Record covers referring to previous record covers?
Yeah – working with Suede and Pulp could be like that. *Coming Up* is not unlike some sort of sixties progressive rock cover. *This is Hardcore* is not unlike a Roxy cover. They're aware of their own pop heritage, and that's part of their art.

There's often an unspoken implication that your work for Factory, and in particular for Joy Division and New Order, is the real Peter Saville. Is this fair?
Yes. I've worked in a lot of different areas, from packaging to television, from fashion to museum, with product, with advertising, with corporate identity, and nowhere have I ever worked the way I did with Joy Division and New Order. I was in an exceptional place doing this work, and it's so totally unrelated to any design experience I've had in any other field. There wasn't anything to do except what I felt like doing. There was nobody to keep happy, because there was a family spirit, and no family member was more important than any other. That is not a situation that I can imagine in any other commercial scenario. Someone might say 'Make me a

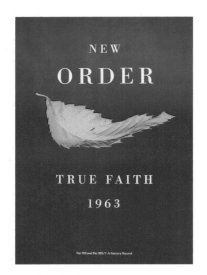

True Faith New Order
Poster 1987
Design PSA and Trevor Key

The Correct Use of Soap Magazine
Virgin album 1980
Design Malcom Garret (*sic*) at Æsthetic Images
Vendôme typeface designed by François Ganeau
in 1952, based on 16*c* Garamond and Jannon

business card, put my telephone number on it, and the rest is up to you.' That card will not be platformed on high streets across the world and delivered to 100,000 people in one month. So not only did I have freedom, I had mass delivery with a core product that the recipient passionately wanted.

I was doing record covers as if they'd be here for all eternity – you can't do graphic design like that. It doesn't work. But I couldn't have done any of those Joy Division or New Order covers to a deadline. Time stood still around my drawing board. I remember an outrageous situation when a proof came back for a *True Faith* poster. I taped it to the wall. There was something wrong with it – a piece of type that was too high. And I sent it back to be done again. Well, you just don't do that in the music industry. The idea of deciding that a piece of type is three centimetres out of place, and that the repro will all be done again, for an in-store poster that will be redundant by tomorrow, is completely out of the question.

Did your approach differ between the two groups?
Joy Division is the human condition more than it is pop. Pop's history is a late fifties one, and the spirit of Joy Division goes outside of that. 'The Coliseum is pretty inspiring, isn't it? Not the Marquee.' For me there are two Joy Divisions. *Unknown Pleasures* is an underpass with iodine streetlights through Manchester at night. *Closer* and *Atmosphere* are the city's gothic revival cathedral and the moors around the Pennines. Manchester was the first industrial city, and even if you don't know that as a kid, you grow up with a certain sensibility.

With New Order there was a little more latitude within which to operate. Had Ian Curtis continued to be there, he would have been the reciprocal figure in the design process. He held the key to what the songs were about. The differences of opinion within New Order created a decision-making void that had to be filled. So the covers are me in conjunction with them. *Republic* is my Los Angeles experience – automatic writing triggered by the songs. I wrote down 'cowboys' when I listened to *Regret* – there's a certain rolling drift. And it's such a lonesome cowboy word: (*wistfully*) 'Johnny regret'.

You once told me that Closer *is mediocre next to Garrett's rather clunky design for Magazine's* The Correct Use of Soap.
Fashion goes through cycles of innovation and retrospection. *Closer* is in a retrospective part of the cycle. *The Correct Use of Soap* is also retrospective, but is innovative with its retrospective material. Malcolm once said to me 'You always take your colours straight from the tube', and I said 'Yeah – you mix yours, and sometimes you make a mess.' And we smiled.

But *The Correct Use of Soap* is innovative – the twist being that you don't normally do that with that kind of typeface. In choosing Vendôme, he picks all the retro classical codes and uses them in a quirky, anarchic, nonclassical way. That's enough. Because it *isn't* the second century BC, and it *isn't* the Coliseum. It's 1980 new wave music. His spirit of assemblage, using classical codes, is much more appropriate.

So you feel that Closer *is more one-dimensional?*
Some sense of *mélange* is carried by the entirety of the product. There's classicism in the typography, neoclassicism in the image and the engraving quality of the paper,

Closer Joy Division
Factory album 1980
Photography Bernard Pierre Wolff
Design Peter Saville and Martyn Atkins

wrapped around a twentieth-century piece of vinyl, on which is the sound and language of 1980. The graphics are purely historical, but the totality is a modern mix. I was contributing an element of the content, not the totality. The cover of *Closer* for a book of nineteenth-century engravings would be very appropriate, and entirely lifeless. No frisson with the content.

If there's a twist to *Closer*, it's that it's a photograph as opposed to an engraving, which is what it's really alluding to. Those Bernard Pierre Wolff pictures are a view on classicism through the contemporary medium of photography. That's what makes it postmodern and *neo*-neoclassical.

The group asked what I had, and I resorted to saying 'I'll show you what I love this month, but I'm sure (*laughs*) it won't be relevant.' Out came Pierre Wolff, and whoa, get out of the way. But what was Ian already thinking? I'm showing them images of tombs because I think they look trendy, and for all I know he's thinking 'That's where I'll write my suicide.' Perhaps if I'd been sent a draft of the lyrics, and had any kind of sensitivity, I might have thought 'I'm not going to indulge that route. Let's have some trees.'

She's lost control/Atmosphere Joy Division
Factory single 1980
Photography Charles Meecham
Typographics Peter Saville

Do your New Order covers constitute your brief autobiography?
Yeah, you can say an awful lot about me and my aesthetic inclinations every year between 1980 and '93 through the New Order covers. To a tee.

Do you take more time over them because they're so synonymous with you?
'Ah, the public will be watching what Saville's up to here …'
There's a little of that. It was my collection, whereas an Ultravox cover is Peter Saville for Ultravox – like John Galliano for Dior, not John Galliano. The visual experience of New Order was Peter Saville. Every other cover I did was for my client, and whether I liked it or not, that was what they'd have. Some of them I don't like at all, whereas with New Order it's 'a Peter Saville-New Order presentation'.

Technique New Order
Flyposting at Factory site 1989
See also p.113

Technique's working title was *Peter Saville's New Order*.
They'd say 'Where's the artwork?' and I'd say 'What's it called?'. Just excuses. (*Mancunian accent*) 'Where's the bloody artwork?' (*exasperated*) 'Well, tell me what you're going to call it, and then perhaps we can start!' 'Ah, yer bastard.' This is the kind of set-up. Rob Gretton, their manager, would press for some titles just to make me do something. They went through titles they liked, and any which hadn't gone on a song were contenders for the album. Rob said 'Why don't we call it *Peter Saville's New Order*, like Andy Warhol's Velvet Underground?' He was serious. I'd been telling him that where Trevor Key and I were going with the dichromats was like Warhol's silkscreening. The group didn't like it.

Would you have liked them to accept that title?
It would have flattered me enormously. But it would have blown my ego out of all proportion, so it's perhaps a good thing that it didn't happen.

You began to turn away from appropriation in the mid-eighties. What did you feel the new direction should be?
1985 is my 'year zero'. This postmodernist layering of retrieved pieces has gone as far as it can go, and is getting quite painful. I bought myself a black polo neck, and I had

The Evil Genius of a King Giorgio de Chirico
1914–15
Polaroid for *Thieves Like Us* New Order
Trevor Key 1984
See also p.87

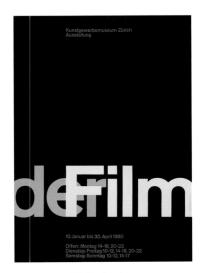

Der Film Josef Müller-Brockmann
Poster 1960

a term, 'essentialism', which became my code within the terms of lifestyle. For me, the retrievalist, nostalgic view that starts in '67 with *Bonnie and Clyde* ends in '85. Trevor and I had long wanted to do a metaphysical piece, and I decided *Thieves Like Us* would be the last piece of straight historical referentialism. 'It's called "Thieves Like Us", so let's just do it.' After that, I'd had enough. I began gently trying to find the future, beginning with *Low-life*.

By this point you'd already determined that no-one needed to see the group themselves, so why resort to that?
It seemed pointless to put yet another façade in front of them. The only thing you could possibly show now was the people who made the music. And there was a novelty to that. Strip the whole lot away, and what are you left with? Four people. Anything else is another conceit, another ism. This was essentialism.

Do you see it as a more honest design than its predecessors?
Well at least it is what it is. I had nothing else to say. It's black and white, Polaroid, not retouched, nothing done to it.

You cloaked it in tracing paper.
I didn't want to put titling on anybody. Put the credits on the tracing paper, it comes away and you've got portraits of the four individuals.

Despite any 'purity' in *Low-life*'s images, its typography still references the past – Josef Müller-Brockmann's *Der Film* poster. It's as if you couldn't completely let go of appropriation.
I couldn't. I'm chronically referential.

Doesn't that dissipate the 'essentialism' of the cover?
No, because at the time it was the first sight we'd had of sixties-style sans serif in pop for some time – before Neville Brody took that approach on *Arena*. It should have been Helvetica or Akzidenz, but I wasn't quite there yet. I used Neuzeit because I felt 'new time'. But to look to Müller-Brockmann in '85 was unusual, because it was still around in the mainstream – timetables and WH Smith still used ranged-left sans-serif. One of the problems with fashion is that it's very difficult to assess out of its time. You have to be in the mindset of that moment to see what the impact is. Using Neuzeit on *Low-life* was shocking – I wouldn't have done it otherwise.

How did essentialism fit your desire to reflect the zeitgeist? Your attempt at stripping away the façade of design occurred in the middle of the most notoriously materialist decade in history!
I was reflecting the direction I felt the zeitgeist would have to take.

As if you were exhibiting consumer bulimia before everyone else?
Yes. That rather childish use of the word 'essential' was to do with the fact that the stylised existence of the early eighties had become confused, and now it was time to raze the field and start again.

Then I began to read about Yves Klein. I'd seen his work but had never understood it. In '85 I pulled the Pompidou Centre's Klein catalogue off the shelf

35

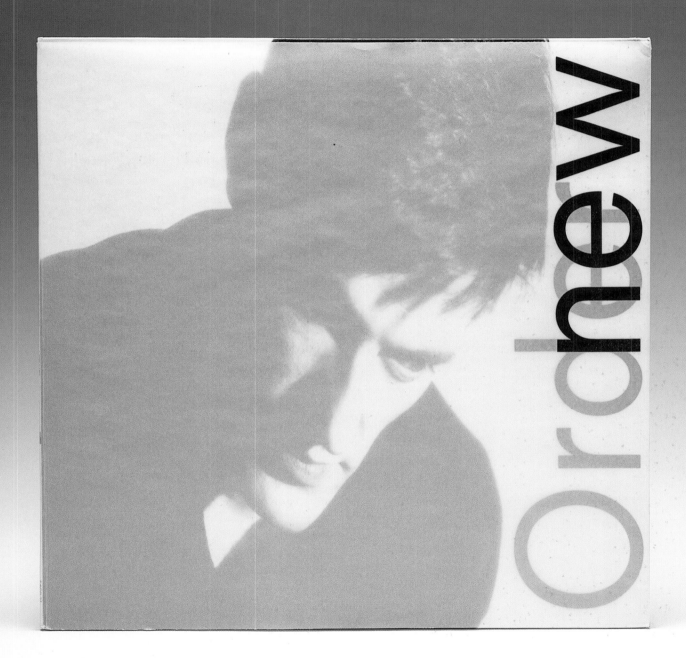

Low-life **New Order**
Factory album 1985
Photography Trevor Key
Design PSA

Untitled Blue Monochrome (IKB 175)
Yves Klein
Dry pigment in synthetic resin on fabric
on wood 1957
©Yves Klein, ADAGP Paris

Peter Saville and Richard Thomas in Lyon
with *Titaanzink* and *Aluchrome* 1987
See p.99–101

First dichromat test 1987
Trevor Key and Peter Saville

Peony 1987
Dichromat Trevor Key and Peter Saville

at my girlfriend's flat, thinking 'Maybe that's something to look at now …'
Talk about essentialism – I was *obsessed* with Klein in '85/'86 – the blue, the gold, the manifestation of nothing, the show called *The Void* – fantastic.

After engaging with a cultural reference on that level, do you file it away in your own past – 'Klein was my 1985 – end of story' – or does it continue to have resonance for you?
You keep it. Unfortunately things do get devalued by people like me, so we'll find pseudo-Klein postcards and bubblebath in shops in Notting Hill, and it all gets trashed. But the essence of Klein is timeless.

If you were to lay out the designs chronologically, would there be a 'before and after *Low-life*' split?
You can see it distinctly. It's still retrievalist, but what happens in '85 is that I pick up the last modern moment. A fifteen-year retrospective period runs from '70 to '85. In '85 I still look back, because I don't know how to go forward, but I look back to the last modern moment of the twentieth century. So instead of de Chirico it's Klein. Instead of early experimental photography it's Bailey's sixties. Instead of romantic nineteenth-century flower painting it's Andy's flowers. In '85 I start playing sixties.

That is still referentialism.
Yes, because that was the only way I knew how to work. But I *felt* that I was being modern. *Low-life* is the manifestation of it. That having been done, you see the little seeds being sown – *Brotherhood* being the first. Not sure what to grow, but I'll just deal with something that *is*. So my Klein colour fields are the sheets of Aluchrome and Titaanzink that Trevor found in the builders merchant's yard. Aluchrome cost £2 a sheet, and seemed more real than Klein's gold leaf. The notion to do something fresh was pushing me. 'Is it a straight reproduction of … ? Then what's the point?' All I've done is go back to a period that I lived through. I didn't partake in it, but I could feel it. Every other period that I'd raided, I didn't have any feeling of. They were all removed. But I knew something of the spirit of the sixties – I knew who the Beatles and Andy Warhol were. Having experienced it 'real time', I couldn't see the point in copying it exactly. So when we start to do stripes in '87, they're like Bridget Riley, but the end result is different. The *Substance* peony is like a Warhol flower, but it's not a Warhol flower. Aluchrome is like Klein, but it's not Klein.

Is it really so significant that now you were making the marks, rather than taking verbatim the marks of someone else?
Yes, because you bring something new to the visual wealth of the world. The peony's still great. All you can say about *Thieves Like Us* is that it's a fabulously clever reassemblage of a painting in photographic form. As a conceit, it's interesting that it's a record cover in 1984. But it's not important. Whereas for me the peony is an important new thing – the world had never had a flower like that before.

Getting Away With It Electronic
Factory single 1989
Design PSA
See also p.119

QJXL New Order
Press advertisement 1989
Quincy Jones anniversary celebration
Design Brett Wickens

New Order Music 1981–89
Songbook image 1990
Photography Geoff Power

Given that you felt 'chronically referential', how did you proceed from your essentialist period?

Post-'85 I had a much greater sense of responsibility, and made some tentative steps forward, picking up where the sixties left off. Ironically, we then get a re-run of the seventies. My first knowingly seventies work is *Getting Away With It*. From this two-year period of feeling modern, I could see that, post-sixties, our culture had drifted hopelessly retro: everything looks a little like something you've already seen, and as a consequence you feel comfortable with the product.

Why take inspiration from an era which was, in your terms, referential first time around?

Having worked through referencing earlier parts of the century, the postmodern cycle had brought me, in the mid-eighties, to the sixties – a genuinely modern era when social change and technological evolution brought about new cultural change. But you've got to keep moving in the cycle, so your retro sixties moment must lead on to a retro seventies moment. But because they're so recent, it becomes difficult to tell the difference between reference and reality. We can go into a contemporary furnished apartment and not know the difference between the nineties stuff and the sixties stuff.

What is the upshot of this trashing of the concept of time?

It's healthy. A good example would be an affluent sixties/seventies Italian domestic interior, where you'd see a hybrid of antiquity and modernity, happily living side by side, not a wall-to-wall fitout in one style, which is rather naïve and culturally insecure. It's nice to see a Barcelona chair next to a bit of Georgian, with late twentieth-century lighting.

But the mixing which you say is healthy still relies on those distinct, extreme aesthetics. You need those Georgians preaching their aesthetic, or for that matter the young Tschichold preaching his Neue Typographie, otherwise you'd have nothing specific to prey on.

But what's nice is to see the individual's ability to live with what's good, rather than to live with any particular moment. It would be psychotic to be only of the moment these days, because the moments move so fast. The breaking down of the time barrier is good because it blurs everything and makes you realise that you exist within a continuum. It's a more healthy way to exist.

Getting Away With It was the first time I used stock photography. The Image Bank had huge archives of seventies material that was so wrong it was right. But I'd become more philosophical – 'What is going on here? Why does this seem right?'

And what was your conclusion?

I read the opening paragraph of Edward Lucie-Smith's 1979 book on hyperrealism, and it could have been written in 1990.[3] 'Wow. 1990 is like 1970 all over again.' It's the calamity at the end of a period of hedonism. The hedonistic progress of the sixties hits a rock-bottom in '69/'70. The hedonistic, credit-rich eighties of Thatcher-era Britain crashes in '89/'90. The conditions are the same, and the mood of the imagery is parallel. I'm still concerned with and orientated around how things look, but a political aspect does come into the work thereafter.

**Fuzzy Logic
Here Comes The Hard Pack
Killer In Drag
Razor Soft
Shot Down In The Surf
Too Hot...Too Big**

Automne Hiver 91–92 Yohji Yamamoto
Advertising copylines 1991
See also p.122

FRANKFURT BALKIND™
PICTURES & PROMISES

Identity proposal
After Jenny Holzer 1994

(new)Order

Recycle New Order
Logo 1998
Art direction Peter Saville
Design Howard Wakefield

I'd always been guided by what I felt, but what I was feeling was aesthetic aspirationalism, for both myself and my audience. In trying to show what a terribly clever person I was, I'd connected with some of the audience. But it was all dressing up: 'What shall we wear to the party?' In 1990 I begin to ask 'Is there a party? And should we go to it?' The Yohji Yamamoto *Game Over* campaign is the first time that I express a political thought, rather than an aesthetic aspiration. Yohji got it. We felt the same. The hedonism had run its course and taken us into recession.

You had been a prominent player in the style culture which *Game Over* was now criticising. Were you setting yourself up?
Game Over is a criticism of design for the sake of consumerism. In the context of Yohji, it was about designer wear, which by the end of the eighties was no longer an end in itself. Fashion's next significant statement was grunge – a total turnaround.

Within *Game Over* there was a statement of transparency. We were setting ourselves up: 'Try to be more honest with the work. Don't dress it up as something it isn't.' What we've seen since is pseudo-realism: 'Let's make it out of MDF and not paint it. Let's design a stencil typeface on the computer.' Decoration by undesign is an even worse state.

Did you follow it up, or is *Game Over* an isolated case?
The *Pictures & Promises* identity proposal for Frankfurt Balkind was another example. They were an agency. It was rather self-effacing, like saying 'We sell bullshit'. My argument was that if people think that advertising is bullshit now, why don't we say it? We'll be respected for self-knowledge and awareness. They didn't use it. In my published work, there are some gentler versions of it – the Waste Paintings are a bit of politics.

But if they are political at all, they're so in a very abstract way. Their aesthetic appeal is far more prominent than any statement they might carry.
Yes, they're a discreet, 'charming' bit of politics. This is the root of my sense of frustration over the last ten years. Not only have I not had an autonomous platform from which to speak, but I've had something other than a look to say. But that message is at odds with any commissioned project I might have. They're not the places to express one's feelings; it's not appropriate. The autonomous zone of a New Order cover might have been the place to say 'Don't we think this looks good at the moment?', but it's not the place to say 'You really don't need this record – it's nowhere near as good as their old ones.'

When you joined Pentagram in 1990, you wanted to make the company 'a bit funkier again. We have to get it how it was in the early 1970s'.[4] But surely the kind of ideas-based work which Pentagram had done in that era was precisely what you'd been rebelling against?
Some of Pentagram's work is fantastic. Theo Crosby had been involved in progressive thinking in architecture, having seen the mistakes of blanket modernism. The first time I saw Ken Grange's 125 train I thought 'Wow, this is so space-age'. Before they formed Pentagram, Fletcher/Forbes/Gill had been the hippest graphics firm in London – they were even photographed in *Vogue*. My contemporaries and I rebelled against what the dynamic of sixties graphics had

41

devolved down into. In the hands of its pioneers, the Saul Bass/Milton Glaser era of graphics was radical. But I grew up surrounded by sentimentalised, cloying misappropriations of what had been a much more vital graphic thought and style. Its moment had passed.

You have to be big for a bank or an airline to come to you. In getting big, all design companies lose the unique skills that got them there in the first place. The brilliance of Pentagram was to construct an organisation that appeared to be big but was in fact human and orientated around the creative abilities of individuals, not another corporate machine itself. The Pentagram structure allowed you to talk from a position of scale and power, but to still be an individual. That's what appealed to me. I was allowed to continue being me.

Channel One
Network title sequence 1992
Design Peter Saville and Brett Wickens

Why didn't it work?
Regardless of any philosophical differences, I didn't have the respect of my partners, because I didn't discipline myself. Also, they had failed to guard against their own obsolescence. I was told that it's written into the Pentagram constitution that a new partner should be made every three to five years, and that that partner should be three to five years younger than the last. When I did a quick tally of the average age around the table, it was fifty-five. I was thirty-five – more than an entire generation out of sync. Pentagram has clung to the image of its founding generation. I was the first of an era that challenged the vision of the founders. So I was out there on my own from a philosophy point, and was hopelessly undisciplined at being part of a team. I double-handicapped myself.

At the same time, you said you were 'trying to understand ideas now, because styling doesn't mean anything any more.'[5] How did you implement that, or didn't it happen?
Having learned how to dress the new era, there was going to be something more called for – some content. Pentagram was one of the schools of functional thinking. I don't know if I can pick any particular thing that was my version of it, but that was the way my work was going.

I'd never had a professional mentor of any sort, so I learned an awful lot, both professionally and philosophically. One of the best quotes ever came in a passing comment from John McConnell one evening, when he was looking at something we were doing. As he turned to walk away he said 'Well, the solution's always in the problem.' I sat down and thought 'What's he saying? "The solution's in the problem"?' It's an enormous foundation stone to fall back on.

It's one of the oldest maxims of design.
I'm sure it is, but I'd never heard it before. Nobody had ever told me such things. I was on my own, with just my assistants, from '80 to '90, and had to learn everything the hard way. Now I had a group of colleagues who had wisdom. There has not been one working day for me since 1993 that I have not fallen back upon something I learned at Pentagram.

You designed *Republic* during that period. It seems a significant break from your previous New Order work – advertising replaces minimalism. Was that the result of your new interest in ideas-based work?

Waste Painting #3 – New Order Covers
Iris print 34 ×34" 2002

Republic New Order
Special edition softpack 1993
See also pp.131–33

Spooky New Order
London single 1994
Preliminary and final designs
Art direction Peter Saville
Digital imaging Paul Brown and Brett Wickens
at FGB West, Los Angeles
Format design Howard Wakefield

Republic is a good example of the wavelength difference at Pentagram – even Alan Fletcher told me that it wasn't graphic design. Conceptually, it's nothing more than the next stop on the circle line of hipness. The 1988 ecstasy thing seemed like the sixties drugs thing, so *Fine Time* and *Technique* are my Warhols. *Getting Away With It* comes in as a recognising moment of the new hipness of seventies. And if the early seventies are your mood board, the West Coast becomes your destination. It's Elliot Gould in *The Long Good-Bye* – that was the movie that I was living in my head, when Brett and I initially went to Los Angeles to work for Channel One. Film noir meets yellow Daytona. *Republic* comes straight out of that.

So you don't consider it a nod to the more ideas-based way of thinking?
It *is* an idea, but I was going that way anyway. New Order work doesn't fall into functionalist ideas; it's more a fantasy.

  Post-Pentagram, my identity proposal for Manchester Records was an idea. What is Manchester? I hadn't lived there for twenty years, and I didn't know. So I asked some people who did. A 'Q & A' session was organised in the Arndale Centre on a Saturday afternoon: people were asked what Manchester meant to them, and sent the answers to me. I chose several, my favourite being 'Guns, drugs & no money'. That's an idea. A similar piece that I learned about at the time was Uwe Loesch's proposal for the city of Leipzig. The city's colours were blue and yellow, and Loesch proposed that on any communications material, a yellow space would be left. The user could put then any image they wanted there – if this person works in Leipzig, they can represent the city however they want.

You've continued to make stylistic pieces as well.
Everything has to be stylistic, but it has to be anchored in an idea. That's the only way that you know when to stop. When you get to the idea that encapsulates the issues, you have the key. Otherwise why is any bit of work better than any other? In my work there has always been an idea.

You said that your work was heading in an ideas direction. It must have been heading there from a more stylistic viewpoint.
This is a reasonable point. (*Pauses*) Somewhere in my four years at college, the penny dropped about how ideas communicate. But my version was more subliminal: the idea could go under the table rather than over. And if you didn't get it, it didn't matter because *it wasn't for you anyway*. The first Factory poster is very clearly an idea. There is a new wave of music which has a hardness to it; it's post-punk. Here's a new industrial, post-punk poster. If you feel somehow attracted to it, you might like what it's telling you about. If you haven't even noticed it, it doesn't matter to you.

  I hadn't been aware that my work *was* ideas-based. Stylisation as an idea was running its course, and we'd have to communicate with some wits again and go direct; to actually 'have an idea' again. It didn't matter how we executed *Guns, Drugs & No Money*. I chose an orange box because the buses in Manchester are orange, but it really didn't matter. You could handwrite it. The thought communicated regardless. That's what became apparent to me as the world styled up, and as stylisation got devalued by people doing it inappropriately.

Manchester Records
Quotes for identity proposal 1995
See also p.146

Compact
Gold leaf on aluminium
Installation detail 1986
White Columns Gallery, New York
See also pp.102–03

Untitled Robert Longo
Charcoal 1981–88
Courtesy of the artist
and Metro Pictures Gallery

Since your Los Angeles experience, you've done even more self-questioning than before. What have been the main strands of that enquiry?
I've seen more clearly what is and is not appropriate. By its very nature, commissioned design work is not an autonomous zone anyway. And even if I had a new autonomous zone, I would question my acts within it in a way that I wouldn't have done twenty years ago.

But presumably you'd always thought you were acting appropriately. It was 'appropriation'.
But if you're driven to get this aesthetic out, that's what is preoccupying you: getting it out.

And that was at the expense of the client's message?
Some of it was just not appropriate. I look at some of those designs now and think 'What kind of infantile mind was at work there?' A lot of the material that I packaged was mediocre, and it had pretentious aspirational packaging to go with it. The fact that a naïve innocent was making that packaging is the only thing that constitutes the fit. I couldn't pitch those products in some pseudo-high-cultural place now. They don't belong there.

But the act of applying high-culture codes to pop-culture products does not necessarily entail pitching those products high. It could be the reverse – a debasement of high culture, like the 'trashing' of Yves Klein which you mentioned earlier.
I was pitching everything as high as I possibly could. But I wasn't analytical. There was a kind of appropriateness, but it was *juvenile*. Bringing some lateral intelligence to what I do is something that's occurred over the last eight years. And it is very much the new contemporary art scene that's made me stop and think 'Well, why did you do that?'

Many of your writings question whether you should now be making art rather than design. When did you first consider making the transition?
I met Robert Longo in the eighties, and saw Joy Division in his work. I saw Ian Curtis on stage in *Men in the Cities*. I couldn't really engage with it in the terms of art theory. But he said to me in '88, 'You make art too.' I thought 'Do I?'
Then in 1994 I was motivated by Tom Solomon to do a show for his gallery, and I had some interesting ideas which came from my everyday life in LA. My last three months there were spent thinking 'What have I been moved by in this place? What have I written notes about and taken pictures of? How might I convert that into something I could put in a gallery?' But when I returned to London, I heard about Marc Quinn's blood head [*Self*, 1991]. I thought, 'If that's the new standard, I'd better go back to my day job'. Even if I'd thought of it, I wouldn't have had anywhere near enough commitment to do that piece. The second period of my work begins at the time of the YBAs. If anything has made me question myself in the last eight years, it's an active contemporary art scene that I could identify with.

45

At Speed Darren Almond and Sarah Morris
Artforum advertisement 2001
Peter Saville and Howard Wakefield

Bus Shelter
Installation 1996
Peter Saville
Part of the Roadworks project
commissioned by FAT

46

Why hadn't the movements you'd quoted in your work, such as Futurism, already had this effect on you?

When you're young, you just *do*. Instinctively. In the second period I began to think about what I might do, and also to think retrospectively about what I had done.

There was great American and European contemporary art in the seventies and eighties, but I didn't have the language abilities for it. I've understood the language of the new British art scene since the last recession because it's the language of English pop. I was drawn to it because its practitioners had been brought up on the same things as me, and I was subsequently to find that some of them were brought up on me.

The question of Peter Saville as artist seems similar to that of Peter Saville as fashion designer. Your work looks like art or fashion; the fact that it isn't either makes it interesting.

The last generation has seen some people working within the discipline of graphics but with their own ideas and opinions to express – Fuel and Tomato being good examples. We see that kind of personality more now. The stumbling block for them is that the graphic communications industry does not provide a platform for it, so they have to publish themselves. So what is that? It's art. There's been a lot of confusion over the topic of authorship in graphic design over the last ten years. There's applied art and fine art. The tools are irrelevant. It's either applied: applied to somebody else's problem or product, or it's fine art: standing alone. The difference is really defined. It's not a grey zone, in my opinion, it's black or white.

I've spent ten years in a fuzzy zone between the two disciplines. I've seen people come and join me there over the years. But you step out into white or black – it's as simple as that. There is nothing to stop anyone from making art. The problem is what you do with it, and in what way it's recognised. You'll ultimately have to engage with the business of either applied art or fine art.

Is fear of making the leap all that has prevented you from declaring yourself an artist?

Not *feeling* that I was an artist was the first impediment. I thought of what I did as playground art, 'art-lite'. But in spirit I was leaning more towards fine art than applied.

But fine art has a different set of values. I understand the values of fashion and communications, rather than the philosophical processes of art. In some ways I have been overly respectful of and intimidated by it, and at the same time superficial about and dismissive of it. I see a lot of work produced under the umbrella of fine art and I'm astonished by its hopelessness. And then there's other work which I find so awe-inspiring that it makes me feel very much a junior, and not in the same league of concept or commitment.

In the late nineties you began to make self-initiated works in the form of the Waste Paintings. Does your application of that work to Gay Dad bridge the gap between fine and commercial art?

Gay Dad is a piece of commercial problem-solving that happened to put to some practical use a technique for which I found a sound rationale. The Photoshop

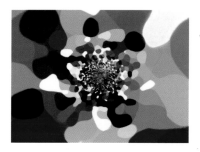

To Earth With Love Gay Dad
London single 1999
Peter Saville, Paul Hetherington
and Howard Wakefield

Made of Waste
Recycled plastic

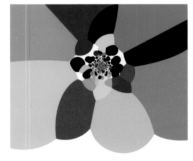

Leisure Noise Gay Dad
Cover and image from London album 1999
Art direction Peter Saville
Logo concept Paul Barnes
Design Paul Hetherington
and Howard Wakefield
See also p.167

'shredding' technique that Paul Hetherington and Howard Wakefield explored had obvious surface appeal, but happened to be a surface-appeal thing that connected with something I felt. There are lots of other good-looking effects filters, but the shredding one had a contemporary rationale.

Was it important to you that the public understood the effect as a recycling one?
Absolutely. The justification for those works is that they have a place *now*. The inspiration behind them is Made of Waste plastic, which looks like Pollock did your kitchen. But it's when you realise what it is that you think 'Oh, that is just so appropriate and fantastic'. It represents the positive, sustainable side of contemporary culture.

That explains the general relevance of recycling, but what made it appropriate for Gay Dad?
It wasn't at all 'appropriate' for Gay Dad. The only demand at the start was that they needed a logo. We arrived at the pedestrian symbol, which was so strong, so total that not only did you not need anything else, it was best not to have anything else. The most you wanted behind that was wallpaper. Anything else would have been confusing and unnecessary. Having made this monumental statement with the figure, could we just then produce a visual-emotional backdrop to any particular track? I didn't want to tell a story about what *Joy* is about; I just wanted to touch the spirit. So we made action paintings that were up or down, simple or complex. They're not thematic; they're purely instinctive. So it's just 'Here's a mood', like choosing what colour lining you might have inside an envelope.

The Waste Paintings were not uncomfortably shoehorned into Gay Dad; they fitted it perfectly. But I won't use the Waste Paintings for something which I don't think they fit.

Are they art?
Yeah, of course.

So that is literally 'applied art'.
Ah no, it's 'art, applied'. And I think there's a difference. The Waste Paintings could be disposable coffee cups. There wouldn't be any harm in that; it would be quite cool. There are probably things that I wouldn't want them to be, but Gay Dad was fine. Nobody said 'Stick this picture of the band alongside the painting' or 'Put this huge bit of lettering on top'. The paintings weren't compromised in any way, so I had no problem with doing it.

When you returned to London in 1994, did you predict that you would have a renaissance?
My feeling through the mid-nineties had been one of fear of being past my sell-by date. I'd plainly failed at Pentagram and at Frankfurt Balkind in LA, to find the safe, natural ground which is the place for rebellious iconoclasts as they get older. That was a really tricky period. I carried on collecting together my thoughts and opinions, wondering 'Is there some private route out of this?' Fortunately, my work has now emerged from the period when it was the last big thing being challenged by the next big thing.

47

Vienna Ultravox
Detail from Chrysalis single 1981
Design Ultravox and Peter Saville
Photograph ©1978 Time-Life Books Inc.

Automne Hiver 91–92 Yohji Yamamoto
Postcard 1991
See also p.122

Touched by the Hand of God New Order
Detail from Factory single 1987
Typography Brett Wickens

You're referring to the 'deconstructionist' generation of David Carson et al.
Yes. The whole Carson nineties era appears, on the surface, to be at odds with my work from the eighties. The *RayGun* aesthetic is a direct affront to it. Which is correct. It has to happen, in the same way that my work was a challenge to that of the era before.

Despite that, pieces such as Republic were seen as relevant alongside the more 'anti-designed' work of the deconstructionists.
Maybe the difference is that my work has some very personal signature qualities, but they're more of a sensibility than a definitive 'look'. I'm an art director-designer, not a mark-making artist. I think conceptually about my times rather than physically-emotionally. So the work I did between 1978 and '93 shifts anyway, because it's an ongoing response to what's needed.

If we take, say, some of the work for Ultravox or OMD – quite preposterous, aspirational, pseudo-cultural posing – by the time of *Game Over* a transition has happened. At one end of the scale I'm saying 'Don't we want life to be perfectly designed?', and ten years later, 'Haven't we had enough of this?' The only real difference between me and the next generation was hands-on practicality.

Those reared on the work of the 1980s 'triumvirate' of Brody, Garrett and yourself were by now grown up. Has that original audience played a significant part in your resurfacing?
This is the most important point pertaining to my work: Malcolm and I, and to some extent Neville, were granted an autonomous zone within pop because it didn't matter. Records were not sold the way soap flakes were sold, so we were given the opportunity.

But we got to do that work in service of another work – the music inside. It was made by young people, on its way to other young people, and into their hearts and minds. That's the key thing. A soap flakes box was never addressed to hearts and minds. But pop music, and particularly subcultural pop music, is a delivery system which goes straight there. It's the single biggest influence on teenagers. Those covers could have been posters or postcards, and a few people might have quite liked them. But without the music it would not have gone to the hearts and minds of hundreds of thousands people.

Young people often grow out of their early influences, and this has doubtless been the case with some of the products you've packaged. What other clues are there to the longevity of the aesthetic?
The bedroom walls of all young people are covered with pictures of the pop stars and groups they love. Then they hit twenty, and all the ephemera of this thing that they loved is put away under the bed, and a year later they throw it out. By abstracting the record cover and bringing cultural references other than a picture of the artist to bear, what Malcolm and I did with covers, and Neville also with *The Face*, was create a visual influence which the recipient could take with them *into their adult life*. Here was a New Order cover, and there was no reason at all why their desk diary, their clothes packaging, or something else beyond music, and which they were now becoming interested in, couldn't look like it. It set new graphic standards for them. Designers before us had done exceptional work for museums, galleries and

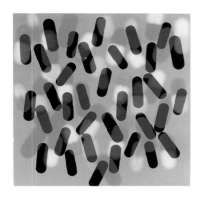

Fine time **New Order**
Factory single 1988
Dichromat Trevor Key and Peter Saville
after a painting by Richard Bernstein
Design PSA
See also p.112

Crystal **New Order**
London promotional single 2001
Art direction Peter Saville
Design Howard Wakefield

other 'worthy' clients who appreciated design, and it was all terribly interesting. But it wasn't hearts-and-minds stuff, and its audience weren't young people in their formative years. People kept the Factory records because they were great works of writing and music. But around them was a vision of how things could be, and I can see now how the sensibility of that audience has been set by it. I meet them now, and now they run companies and are organising or curating. Nobody papers their bedroom with IBM posters. It's a different mindset: it's obsession.

I can't separate the icon of *Blue Monday* from *Blue Monday*. You could take that cover and put in an ineffective pop song and it would still look good, but it wouldn't be an icon. *Blue Monday* is a landmark in pop music. The opportunity is there for the visual aesthetic to make an imprint upon the mind. If the music doesn't open the mind up then you're not making the imprint, and if the cover isn't up to much, not much is imprinted. In a poster shop, *Marilyn* is merely a nice image. But in the context of the world of Andy Warhol …

You said that you used to work instinctively, so presumably you weren't consciously making a formative impression on that audience.
No, I was doing what I wanted. There was a temporary autonomous zone, and within it I created a world as I wanted it to be.

The influence comes later, when that imprint seeps out and we see that the communications world around us has shifted. It's not particularly about graphics, it's about a converging of different strands of influence. It's about positioning things in the broader scheme of our popular culture. My contribution has been to place print within the context of other things that we live with – to see it as something which sits alongside our car, our wardrobe, our furniture. 'How can I make an interface for this product, and fit it into the scheme of things?' It's the chessboard of lifestyle.

When we look at typography on records now, some 8-point Helvetica is considered quite adequate. Fifteen years ago, 'Well, sorry, but that's spine copy and the name and title must occupy the top third of the cover'. When I drive by an Audi advert made solely of coloured stripes, that's when I think, 'Okay, that's big influence'. Even just one cover such as *Blue Monday*, twenty years ago, starts a chain reaction. The real influence has taken a decade-and-a-half to impact – for the people who grew up on it to become the opinion-formers of a later period.

49

1 *Eye* no.17, vol.5, summer 1995, p.13

2 Jon Pareles 'New Order keeps marching to its own mystery'
The New York Times, 12 February 1989

3 Edward Lucie-Smith *Super Realism*, Phaidon, Oxford 1979

4 & 5 *Blueprint*, November 1990, p.30

There[1] was[2] a[3] time[4] when[5] the[6] only[7] art[8] I[9] had[10] on[11] my[12] walls[13] was[14] by[15] Peter Saville[16]

Paul Morley

1 The work of Peter Saville that I like best is the work that really places you there, there where you should be, there inside the work, inside the work that the design, the thoughts, the decisions, are wrapping, interpreting, enhancing, positioning. When his designs put you right there, a there where ideas are smart, bold, old and new, a there where a mind meets an outside world on the inside, where art meets commerce, where space meets time, where there and then meet there and now, then you are exactly where you should be, in the centre of the there that there is whenever form embraces content and vice versa, wherever the visual collapses into the linguistic, whatever there is where text, type and technology are made to spatially co-ordinate, the there where Saville actually removes himself from the act of designing and doesn't really do anything at all.

2 What was so great about the early work of Saville, when he was working for Factory, and DinDisc, even Ultravox, hardly Wham though (I think around here there should be a !), that period that was between say 1978 and 1985, when he was mostly a designer of record sleeves that you were tempted to applaud whenever you saw them, was that his designs were so entertaining and eclectic they were simply unlike anything else in the pop world, and he was himself using these sleeves to develop a narrative that was his own personal history of graphic design. As he drew out this narrative, he added to the history, and took the history down new twists and turns. He was part of design history and he was outside design history. He was academic and aesthete. Student and guru. Peter Saville, for a time, was a genius, which is not to say he isn't one now, just that you only really notice that he was a genius because of the way his twenty-year-old work does not look twenty

PS 1978
Photography Peter Saville

So Peter Gabriel
Detail from Virgin album 1986
Typography Brett Wickens

The Factory
Poster 30×40" 1978
Design Peter Saville

years old, but somehow a hundred years old and/or a day old and yet something out of now or tomorrow. He was great because the designs that are now 'was' still have considerable power beyond the product they were promoting, packaging, branding, disguising, revealing. What was relevant at the time now has a modern relevance as a sign of mental sophistication that has little to do with the fashion of the times. His work has crossed the abyss of time, and remains interesting to look at and think about. The passage of time often makes commercial work wither into its time. Saville's never belonged fully to the time it apparently appeared and represented, so it has never really been required to stick there. It was in the past, but it connected to other periods, which perhaps accounted for why at the time it seemed so unique. He was capturing essence, which went beyond the time and space of any particular fashion. What he was originating back in the seventies, the eighties, the period when he was obviously classic, was not itself the destination, it was the means of travel.

3 Until Peter Saville I had never really considered the kind of mental energy, the poetic vividness, the balanced exuberance that there could be simply in fashioning, positioning, isolating, imagining, worshipping, neglecting, manipulating, loving the letter 'a', let alone the twenty-five or so other letters in the alphabet. Saville could take the letter 'a', and in a matter of time, with the help of a little space and surface, produce a piece of work that said quite a lot about the fragile, preposterous dynamics of existence. With just one use of an 'a' Saville was confirming what he believed in – the fact that faced with the difficulty of believing in anything we have to believe in something so we might as well believe in the letter a, without which language is only a fraction of what it could be. It was also always exciting seeing him put a with b, just for the sake of going from a to b. Sometimes he would borrow an a and borrow a b but the way he mixed the a with the b was totally original. And then there was his ability to mix a and b using different letters altogether. With Peter Gabriel's *So* he was able and willing to make an erotic corporate logo out of a two-letter word while using conflicting typefaces, something I've always felt was the graphic design equivalent of a great richly minimal Miles Davis solo. Saville's technique, or trick, of estimating the exact distance between a letter and some white space was always very impressive.

4 We can detect from Saville's relationship to time just what his relationship is to reality. He considers reality something that must be improved at all cost, and oddly enough this is how he perceives time – as something that isn't all that it seems, as something that can actually be improved. He treats time very seriously, as you can see from his work, which is all about time. He treats time so seriously that he makes up his own version of time. He reproduces time in two-dimensional form. He understands time only too well, which is why he tends to be in time, if not on time.

5 I remember when I first saw the sleeve for Joy Division's *Unknown Pleasures*. With such a sleeve there was no way the music could not be important. Whatever group of people had come to the conclusion that the album sleeve was going to be so symbolic, secretive and madly composed, were clearly involved in something strangely new. It was a surrealistically sensible and deeply appropriate design, the last thing you might have imagined at the time, thinking of what else was around, thinking even of the Bowie/Kraftwerk/Roxy things that had inspired the group,

USE HEARING PROTECTION

MAY 19-THE DURUTTI COLUMN/JILTED JOHN

MAY 26-BIG IN JAPAN/MANICURED NOISE

THE FACTORY

JUNE 2-THE DURUTTI COLUMN/CABARET VOLTAIRE

JUNE 9-THE TILLER BOYS/JOY DIVISION

RUSSEL CLUB ROYCE RD MOSS SIDE

Unknown Pleasures Joy Division
Factory album 1979
Design Joy Division and Peter Saville

but as soon as you saw it, it was absolutely the only sleeve possible. It was visual sound, processed memory, static movement, collapsed space, smooth friction, tuned time, detailed nothing, and it helped create the reality whereby the group could be perceived as truly great.

6 Saville never really worked well with groups or products that began with 'the'. He worked best when there was a space where 'the' might have been, in a time before and after 'the', in a way that avoided 'the', for reasons that have something to do with a sentence that begins with 'the.'

7 Only time will tell if Saville will ever actually finish what he started. The Factory list, the collection he inspired, the order he made happen, the art and the numbers, were like his *Citizen Kane*; he did so much so early, and along the way, obviously, there has been his *F for Fake*, and his *Macbeth*, and his *Touch Of Evil*, and there have been voice overs, hack work and ad work, but you tend to wonder if he'll ever get a chance to produce his *Don Quixote*, if he'll ever get to finish his history, or did he finish it when no-one was looking, and after all that appearance, that manipulation of appearance, the thing he has achieved is a disappearance, as part of his history, his imaginative history of design history. He changed everything to such an extent there was no room left for anything else. He changed the look of things so that he could find somewhere to hide.

8 a/ The art of seeing things that are invisible.
   b/ The art of seeing that rescues the existence of things.

9 For Saville there is only one I in the Universe, and it is his I, the I of the form, the I in the ego, the I for an I, the I which everything revolves around, the I of Saville, the I in his smile, which is an I for a story, the story of I, the designing of a designed world he wants his I to occupy and patrol.

10 I'm not sure if Wham had Saville or if Saville had Wham, but either way this sentence finishes with a !

11 On reflection, it is a shame that Benetton or Nike or Mercedes-Benz didn't turn out to be the Factory of Saville's later life.

12 My feeling is that Saville found ways to work for other people and create something that was all about him, whilst also being representative of his client, so that he created a series of portraits that capture both the illusion of the subject, their different stages, as well as the illusion of his own personality, his own shifting moods, emotional needs and changing skills. There are also various grades and shades of reality connecting him to the illusion of his work, a lot of them to do with his sense of history, his sense of humour, his nerve, and basically his taste, which controls him.

13 In fact, I don't usually like having art on my walls, and at the moment, I have no art on my walls. They are bare. They are waiting for Godot. But once upon a time, I had some Saville-designed posters on my wall, and as far as I was concerned, they

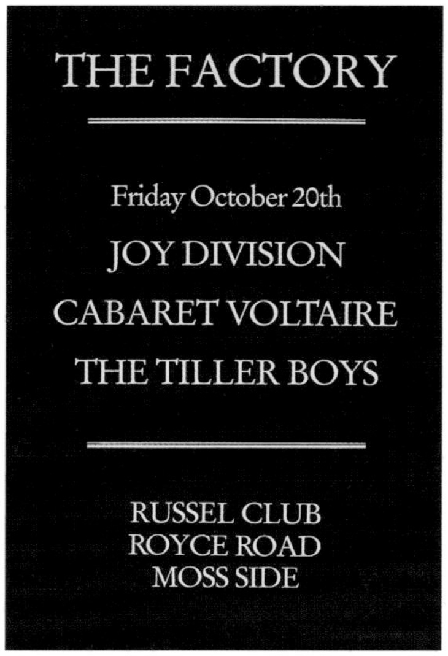

THE FACTORY

Friday October 20th

JOY DIVISION

CABARET VOLTAIRE

THE TILLER BOYS

RUSSEL CLUB
ROYCE ROAD
MOSS SIDE

The Factory
Poster 20×30" 1978
Design Peter Saville

were art, and Saville was an artist. I had two posters on my wall, a black and white poster advertising a gig at the Factory club in Manchester, and a yellow and white poster advertising another gig at the same place. They were in fact just a list of names, an arrangement of type, text and space reminding me of a time to come, or a time that had passed, actually the time of an event, but even though they as such lacked an image, lacked any kind of imagery, they seemed to me to be art. They were the beginning of Saville's history, and it was a history that began very calmly, and with unbelievable belief in simplicity and the future, and indeed the past and the present.

14 See number two. Note also that the device used in the writing of this essay was first employed by J G Ballard in the seventies, and I have appropriated it in much the same way that Saville would take an image or a style or a theory from the past and change it by applying it elsewhere, in another time zone, in another context, in another sense, as if to say, nothing is new, unless you say that it is, and you really believe in what you say, up to a point.

15 Each piece of design by Peter Saville that makes up the idea of what it is that he is designing is really a part of his ongoing search as to what exactly a graphic designer is. Every design by Peter Saville is a question about itself that supplies a kind of answer. Anything by Peter Saville is a particular solution to a specific question that he then turns into a new question, a question usually to do with himself, and his own value to himself, and the outside world.

16 Peter Saville has always been designed by Peter Saville.

FAC–2

A FACTORY SAMPLE

A Factory Sample Various artists
Factory EP 1978
'Packaged by Peter'

Electricity
Orchestral Manoeuvres in the Dark
Factory single 1979
Design Peter Saville

The Factory
Poster 20×30" 1978
Design Peter Saville

THE FACTORY

December

7th
THE ADVERTS

8th
DISTRACTIONS

9th
THE DOOMED

15th
MANICURED NOISE
HUMAN LEAGUE

16th
MAGAZINE

18th
MESSAGANA
ALPHA OMEGA

21st
UNDERTONES

22nd
CHRISTMAS PARTY

RUSSEL CLUB
ROYCE ROAD   MOSS SIDE

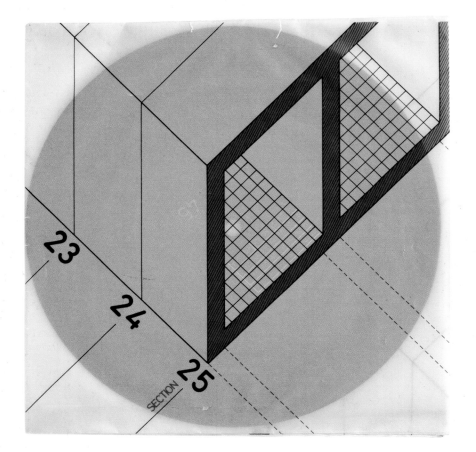

Girls Don't Count Section 25
Factory single 1980
Design Ben Kelly and Peter Saville

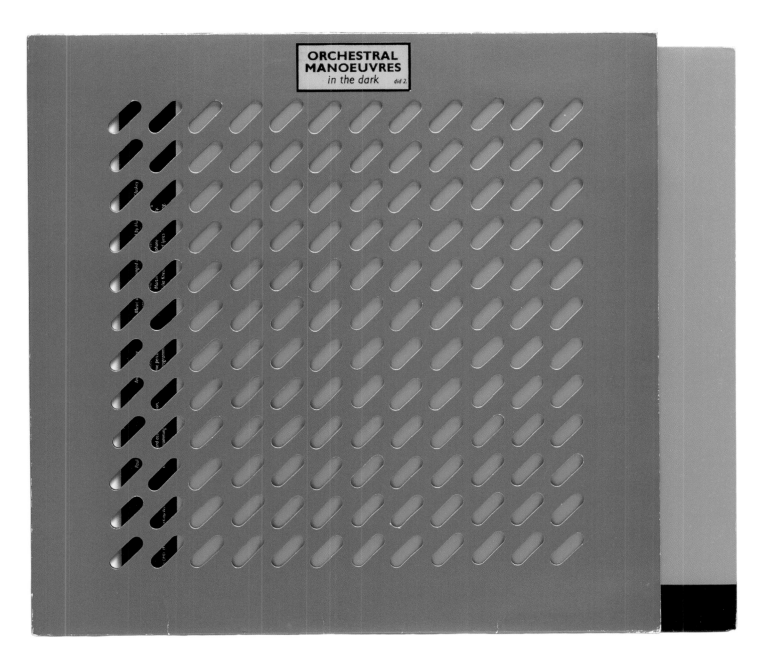

Orchestral Manoeuvres in the Dark
DinDisc album 1980
Design Ben Kelly and Peter Saville

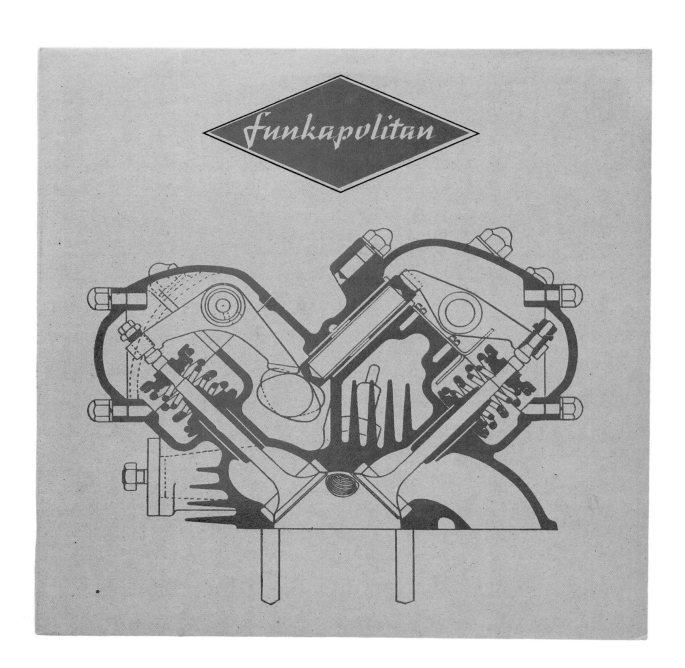

Funkapolitan
Decca album 1982
Design Peter Saville and Funkapolitan
Illustration Phil Irving/Albion Scott Ltd
Logotype Geoff Halpin
Artwork Brel Wik, Grafica Industria g11
Issued in two colourways

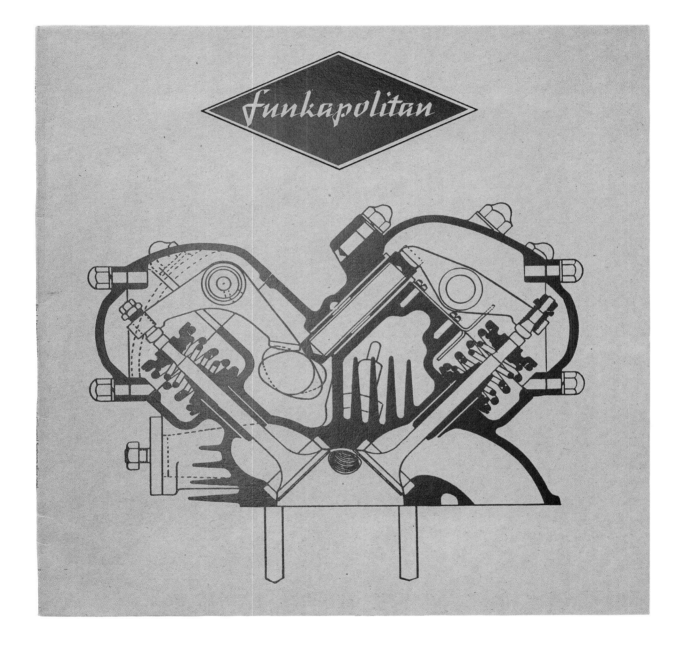

Love Will Tear Us Apart Joy Division
Factory single 1980
Photography Trevor Key
Design Peter Saville

Metal Lined Cubicles
Ben Kelly thesis cover
Royal College of Art 1974

Still Joy Division
Factory album 1981
Design Grafica Industria

Ceremony New Order
Factory singles 1981
Design Peter Saville and Brett Wickens
Albertus type specimen
Design Berthold Wolpe 1937

68

Everything's Gone Green/Procession **New Order**
Factory single 1981
Design Peter Saville and New Order
Issued in nine colourways
Dynamo by Fortunato Depero 1927

Movement New Order
Factory album 1981
Design Peter Saville and Grafica Industria
Futurismo
Journal cover Fortunato Depero 1932

OMD

SOUVENIR & MOTION & HEART AMAZON VERSION & SACRED HEART. C 1981 DIN 24

Producer – M. Howlett. Zincografica SpA   DINDISC   61 - 63 Portobello Road, London W11 3DD.

Souvenir Orchestral Manoeuvres in the Dark
DinDisc single 1981
Design Peter Saville and Brett Wickens
Location shot from *Souvenir* **video**
OMD driving Saville's Karmann Ghia

& MORALITY

by
Orchestral
Manœuvres
In The Dark

ARCHITECTURE

71

Architecture & Morality
Orchestral Manoeuvres in the Dark
DinDisc album 1981
Design Peter Saville and Brett Wickens
Architectural photography Robin Roddey

A change of speed,
a change of style

Rick Poynor

It may seem strange to anyone who is not a graphic designer, but album cover design has never been highly regarded within the design profession. General histories of the subject never show many of them. Those that sneak in were often created by people whose reputations in other areas of graphic design are already secure. There was always a feeling among the more hard-nosed kind of design professional that music graphics were not entirely serious. Design was about 'problem solving' and in the case of a cover design for a rock or pop group, there wasn't much of a problem to solve. It all seemed rather easy compared to grappling with a corporate identity for a multinational, or churning out sample brochures for a paint manufacturer. There was also, perhaps, an element of envy. To judge by the results of their handiwork – and this is going back two or three decades before the marketing departments got their cold, calculating hands on everything – record sleeve designers appeared to be allowed to do what they liked. They hung out with musicians and the whole arrangement looked uncomfortably close to art.

It was certainly true that record sleeve designers were a different breed. They tended, in the best cases, to be specialists and they often loved both the music and its milieu. In other words, they were much like the audience. Some were literally super-fans – people who had found a way to get even closer to the thing they craved. This high degree of emotional investment is what makes music design so fascinating. A Dulux brochure from the seventies might have slight interest as part of a significant designer's oeuvre. It might tell a researcher something about patterns of taste and consumption at the time. It might even be a highly accomplished piece of design. But it has no wider, lasting interest, and beyond its ephemeral function it will never have meant much to anyone. By contrast there has never been a form

The West Shore 1999
Photography Peter Saville

Maid of Orleans
Orchestral Manoeuvres in the Dark
Poster 1981
Design Brett Wickens
Photography Robin Roddey

Peter Saville, Tony Wilson and Alan Erasmus
outside The Factory
Photography Kevin Cummins 1978

Women Around the World at Work
Martha and the Muffins
DinDisc single 1981
Design Brett Wickens

of graphic communication so densely charged with private signals, so personal and intimate, or so inseparably fused to the sense of who you are, as the album cover. Posters come close, perhaps; you live with them and they become part of the scenery of your life. Book covers, as graphic objects, have something in common. There is a sense of physical connection: you handle the book to read it, though once it is finished and shelved it may never be looked at closely again. But book cover designs are not tethered to their contents and no one minds too much when they are periodically revamped. With twelve-inch record sleeves, it was quite different. Whenever you played an album, the cover made a reappearance. Naturally, the music was the point of the exercise, but precisely because the musical experience was so intense and meaningful, the packaging that housed it became an object of desire. Its large size helped to make it a mood-setter, a contemplative aid, a vivid statement of artistic intent in its own right. Flipping through the racks in a record shop, it was often the first thing you absorbed about an album. Pink Floyd's *Atom Heart Mother* (1970) was that cow in the field. The Mothers of Invention's *Weasels Ripped my Flesh* (1970) was that grinning idiot mutilating his face with a weasel-razor. And Joy Division's *Unknown Pleasures* (1979) will always be those mysterious, white waveforms set with hair-raising precision in a pool of inky blackness.

Peter Saville is unusual among designers who came to fame by creating album covers in never seeming to care that much about the music, even if he enjoyed the scene. It is hard to find an early interview in which he mentions the music as sound. He liked Orchestral Manoeuvres in the Dark, but appears to have had mixed feelings about early Joy Division, though he recognised *Unknown Pleasures* as an important record. Certainly he never came across as a rock and roll person or a fan. Yet that slight detachment – even though he sought out Tony Wilson to offer his services and became a founding partner of Factory – was central to what he achieved. His work's strength lies in its sense of remove. As a direction, it was planned, analytical and deliberate. Saville realised, while still at Manchester Polytechnic, that the look of the mid- to late seventies had run its course and that something had to replace it. 'I thought that, for a piece of work to stand out from the rest, it would have to go quite a different way, and be very disciplined and very ordered', he said in 1981. Paradoxically, this meant producing work that bore a striking resemblance, in form and methodology, to the problem-solving approach of formal graphic design (his tutors were apparently puzzled by this unexpected turn of events). It was extraordinary, in 1979, to see such an austere, reductionist approach applied to the wild terrain of the rock album cover, on which music fans were accustomed to expect anything and everything except fastidious restraint. It was a powerful repudiation of punk's clamour that no one could miss, and the mark of an aesthetic sensibility that was excitingly unfamiliar in rock. It gave Factory a perhaps undue appearance of avant-garde seriousness and conceptual rigour. *Unknown Pleasures* was one of those rare, startling and unforgettable covers that inspired young people to take up design.

Saville has never made any secret of the fact that in his earliest sleeves he was completing his design education in public. His friend, Malcolm Garrett, had introduced him to Herbert Spencer's book, *Pioneers of Modern Typography*, an inspiration on his own early design work, and Saville was particularly attracted to Jan Tschichold's later classical phase. His most memorable early sleeves are usually responses of one kind or another to aesthetic and historical discoveries, and they

Detail from **Berthold Type Catalogue**
See pp.76–77

Metro Music **Martha and the Muffins**
DinDisc album 1980
Cover concept Martha and the Muffins
Sleeve based on Map 30 M/11
of the National Topographic System
with kind permission of Department
of Energy, Mines and Resources,
Ottawa, Canada

Reference for *Blue Monday*
See p.79

tend to involve the transposition of unexpected and even dissonant material into the pop music context. The source could be something as simple as a map (for Martha and the Muffins), a perforated metal grill (Orchestral Manoeuvres in the Dark), or a floral fabric sample (also for OMD). Saville's intimation – inspired by postmodern architecture – that neoclassical imagery was right for Joy Division's second album, *Closer* (1980), was a double-sided example of his prescience. It signalled Factory's awareness of broader cultural tendencies in the visual arts, but it also acquired a second, unforeseen meaning. By the time the album appeared, Ian Curtis had killed himself and the white sleeve, cold as a block of ice, with lettering based on second-century BC Roman stone-carvings, looked like a memorial. Bernard Pierre Wolff's photograph of a mourning scene in a crypt only added to the funereal impression, yet everything had been agreed with Curtis and the band weeks before his death.

Later, Saville got into trouble for failing to acknowledge the Italian Futurist Fortunato Depero as the direct source for the covers of New Order's *Movement* and *Procession*. He always insisted it was the band who didn't want to run the credits and this rings true because right from the start he thought like a fashion designer or trend forecaster. His method, then as now, lies in fixing on a style or look slightly ahead of popular taste. You need to know and appreciate the sources to grasp the astuteness of his acts of selection and he readily obliged. In an early interview, he lays out his references with the confident precision of a forecaster showing mood boards at a client presentation. Section 25's *Always now* (1981) is based on the Berthold type catalogue and the work of Jan Tschichold. The typeface is Bembo – typeface choice has always been fundamental to Saville's perception of cultural mood-shifts – and the blue-marbelled cover board, if you were asking, is courtesy of La Ste. Keller-Dorian Papiers in France. Reference material for OMD's *Architecture & Morality* (1981) includes Herbert Bayer and the Bauhaus, British institutionalism of the thirties, and photographers and designers of the Modern Movement. The Toronto map reference for Martha and the Muffins' *Metro Music* (1979) is Map 30M/11 of the National Topographic System, Department of Energy, Mines and Resources, Ottawa. Enough to satisfy even the most determined source-tracker.

These packages were immensely seductive, but in the age of the CD, with vinyl now largely the preserve of collectors, it is easy to lose sight of the fact that twelve-inch record sleeves, as a medium, were always seductive. The gatefold sleeve, which had more or less disappeared by the time Saville arrived, was an expensive and wastefully luxurious item. Designers had also been experimenting for years with the standard slipcase. Saville productions such as *Always Now*, constructed like an envelope, or New Order's *Blue Monday* twelve-inch single, die-cut to resemble an early floppy disk, were lavish, but other record companies also produced lavish packaging. What set Saville's designs apart from most of the competition was that they were conceptually lavish, too. At times it could feel as though design, rather than music, had become the most significant aspect of the enterprise and this led to complaints about over-design – as when Jon Savage accused the Section 25 cover of swamping the band's tentative music. In the case of *Blue Monday*, though, the hugely confident, wordless, five-colour cover, with black inner sleeve, was brilliantly appropriate to a sequencer-generated track that fused rock and dance rhythms to define and popularise a new sound. Once again, the design had an art historical

Section 25–Always now friend
ly fires dirty disco c.p. loose tal
k costs lives inside out melt clos
e hit babies in the bardo be bra
ve new horizon produced by
martin hannett engineer joh
n caffrey recorded at brittania
row disegnatori : grafica indu
stria e typografica berthold a
factory records product fact 45

16.5 mm (60p)   10   20

Section 25

DESIGN : GRAFICA INDUSTRIA
MARBLED PAPER Nº 93B
REPRODUCTION AUTORISÉE PAR
LA STE. KELLER – DORIAN
PAPIERS. F R A N C E

FACTORY
COMMUNI
CATIONS
LIMITED

Power, Corruption and Lies New Order
Factory album label 1983
Based on Diatronic typesetting disc
Typography Peter Saville

source, in this case Claes Oldenburg's over-scaled, pop art drum kits and telephones. Saville caught something in the air and gave it the solidity of an icon. His related, rose-festooned cover for *Power, Corruption and Lies* (1983) – one of the most left-field images ever to grace a rock record – shows how sure-footed his borrowings had become. It is doubtful that many New Order fans would have known much about Fantin-Latour or enjoyed the image as an oil painting. Everything depends on the sense of contextual displacement, intensified by the colour code used on the back cover, on the inner sleeve, and in the corner of the painting itself. Not for the first time, Saville achieved the sort of ambiguity and complexity of resonance more usually associated with art.

Saville's long-lasting relationship with Joy Division/New Order might seem to confirm a mainstream designer's worst prejudices about record cover design. As he has often noted, once the band trusted him, they left him to decide what to put on the sleeve. With the wrong designer, this might have been a recipe for disaster. In Saville's case, the degree of freedom inspired much of his finest work. Far from being wilful, *Blue Monday* shows a disciplined understanding of both content and audience. Anything but an exercise in superficial styling – the constant complaint about eighties design – it is first and foremost a graphic idea. (It wasn't surprising that these qualities eventually led to a partnership offer from Pentagram, home of 'idea-based' design.) The fact that there is still so much interest in Saville's work from these years shows there are moments when, if only designers were given a freer hand, exceptionally compelling design could result.

Over the last twenty years, designers have constantly complained, to anyone who will listen, about the way in which their scope to determine visual directions has been eroded by marketing. Saville, too, has struggled to find the freedom he had at Factory. In the music business, superb design now happens against the odds. The quest for certainty and sales volume leads to control of the risk-factor on which creativity depends – and these commercial anxieties do have a point. Owing to high production costs, the original version of *Blue Monday* lost money. Factory eventually overstretched itself and failed. Perhaps it could never have been otherwise, when the gesture of making the work trumped all other concerns, but this idealism imbued the best of these records and sleeve designs with something truly special in the ephemeral worlds of pop music and packaging: the power to last.

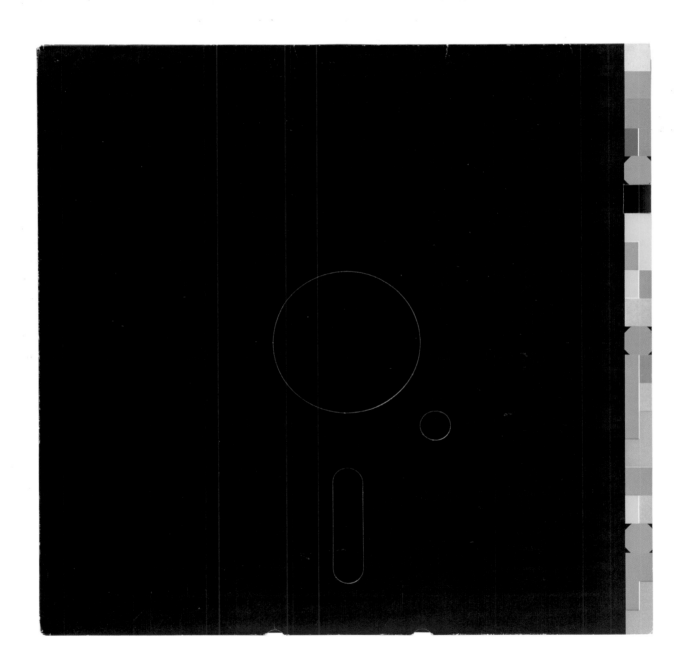

79

Blue Monday New Order
Factory single 1983
Design Peter Saville and Brett Wickens

Power, Corruption and Lies **New Order**
Factory album 1983
Design PSA
A Basket of Roses Henri Fantin-Latour 1890

Confusion **New Order**
Factory single 1983
Design PSA

The Haçienda first anniversary
Poster 30×40" 1983
Design PSA

FAC 51 MAY 21 I YEAR

HAÇIENDA

84

From the Hip Section 25
Factory album 1984
Photography Trevor Key
Design PSA

86

Talking Loud and Clear
Orchestral Manoeuvres in the Dark
Virgin single 1984
Design PSA
Fabric supplied by Monkwell Fabrics CR 4015

Thieves Like Us New Order
Factory single 1984
Photography Trevor Key
Design PSA

Gravitas and grace

Peter Hall

Back in the mid-eighties, as Peter Wollen noted in his introduction to the 1998 exhibition catalogue *Addressing the Century*, Yohji Yamamoto was one of a triumvirate of Japanese designers to be instigating a kind of revival of nineteenth-century Arts and Crafts philosophy on the western catwalks. Alongside Issey Miyake and Rei Kawakubo at Comme des Garçons, Yamamoto brought craftsmanship and an experimental approach to materials to the cutting table. (At the time, London and Paris were largely preoccupied with the symbolism of street style and redefining gender roles through clothing.) Equally important, the big Japanese three had an expansive view of what actually constitutes the fashion show. Wollen notes that Kawakubo, the first to arrive, tended to see her clothes as 'elements in a total environment', reflecting her approach in her accessories, shows and shops.

It was in this context that the *haute couture* catalogue emerged. Comme des Garçons extended its image to print with its esoteric *Six* magazine, and Yamamoto assigned a sizeable budget and open remit to art director Marc Ascoli to produce a limited edition catalogue aimed at a select list of people. After a handful of seasons featuring upcoming photographers like Max Vadukul, Ascoli turned to Nick Knight, whose black and white portraits he had seen in *i-D* Magazine. The choice of a photographer from an emerging street fashion magazine was deliberate. '*Vogue* and *Elle* weren't running the show anymore,' recalls Knight. 'The more funky designers working at the time like Yohji, Rei Kawakubo, Jean-Paul Gaultier and Martine Sitbon actually wanted the audience that was reading *i-D* and *The Face*.'

At Knight's suggestion, Saville was brought in to design the autumn/winter 1986–7 catalogues. At the time, Saville represented an approach somewhat against the grain in the world of graphic design, which was sporting layered, 'deconstructed'

Printemps Eté 87 Yohji Yamamoto
Catalogue cover
Art direction Marc Ascoli
Photography Nick Knight
Design PSA

Printemps Eté 88 Yohji Yamamoto
Catalogue cover
Art direction Marc Ascoli
Photography Nick Knight
Design PSA

Automne Hiver 86–87 Yohji Yamamoto
Image from catalogue cover
Art direction Marc Ascoli
Photography Nick Knight

layouts sprinkled with idiosyncratic and historicist motifs. If its motive, to upturn the monumental authority of modernism, was valid, Saville considered its means tiresome. 'I was tired of meaningless reference,' he says. 'I wanted something essential.'

The first Saville/Knight/Ascoli catalogues for Yohji Yamamoto were shot in black and white, with one splash of colour – on the cover of the women's catalogue – in a bright red bustle. The black silhouettes and stripped out white backgrounds made a stark contrast to the tropes at work in mainstream fashion photography: a comparable *Vogue* shoot by Patrick Demarchelier finds his models *en plein air*, their slick, shiny flesh set against the scenery of the Moroccan desert, or gazing across the ocean. But sexually-charged atmospherics were strikingly absent from Knight's shots, which had more in common with David Bailey's vibrant portraits of the swinging sixties. They made no attempt at the pretence of a setting, nor an appeal to some fantasy narrative. Saville's pacing and arrangement of the images further emphasised the strangeness of the shapes made by the dressed bodies. This was bare bones image-making, in which the model became a malleable graphic form.

The challenging caveat of the Yamamoto account was that Knight was required to think anew each season. Yamamoto maintained a distance from the process, offering only minimal maxims like 'surprise me' (according to Saville) and 'show me my dreams' (according to Knight), while Ascoli would 'goad' Knight into challenging his own preconceptions. Knight's response was to strenuously experiment with shooting and processing techniques. The camera, film and processing became, in Knight's hands, less tools than paints. With the summer 1987 catalogue, he and London lab BDI introduced the strangely blown-out 'cross-processed' colour that quickly became *de rigeur* in editorial and subsequently advertising for the duration of the decade. Achieved by running transparency film through a bath of negative developing fluid, it had an effect reminiscent of a television screen with the colour contrast on full; mid-tones disappeared leaving highly saturated, glowing colours.

For Saville, Yamamoto's hands-off creative direction and spare-no-expense approach to craftsmanship provided a unique opportunity to indulge his creative instincts. The women's catalogue from spring/summer 1988 gave a slight nod in the direction of Kubrick's *2001: A Space Odyssey*, with white Yamamoto hats floating like spacecraft across a smooth surface of smooth, deep, black ink. The black cover featured no type, forming an impassive monolith alleviated only by the hint of deep red solar flares, bleeding off the edge and spilling into the exaggerated colours of the models – who floated, like the hats, on blackness. 'The catalogue production was exemplary,' says Saville, who adds that Yamamoto's organisation only questioned his design specifications once, when Saville called for black thread-sewn pages in the outer space catalogue. 'I received a fax from the head of production,' he says. 'It said: "Black thread not possible".' Instead they sought out black staples.

Throughout the five seasons in which Knight, Ascoli and Saville worked together, the catalogues had a consistently reductive, pared-down appearance – conveying Yamamoto's sense of refinement, almost to the point of aloofness. The sensibilities contributing to the task seemed particularly well matched: Knight's photographs, which frequently explored and tested visual extremes, were presented in Saville's quietly lyrical settings. Design became present only in the absence of design.

92

Automne Hiver 87–88 Yohji Yamamoto
Advertisement
Art direction Marc Ascoli
Photography Nick Knight
Design PSA

Automne Hiver 88–89 **Yohji Yamamoto**
Images from catalogue
Art direction Marc Ascoli
Photography Nick Knight
Design PSA

Automne Hiver 91–92 **Yohji Yamamoto**
Postcard 1991
See also p.122

Saville sees his work for Yamamoto as one of providing a 'discreet pedestal'. He adds, 'It lionises the work'. Knight offers an alternative take: 'I'm in awe of the refinement and the modernity Peter can bring to something. There's a sort of hurt artist in him, a certain sadness in what he does that gives it gravitas. He also removes things to try and find out what the core values are, and I think he does that in a very beautiful way. Without him, the catalogues probably would have looked the same, but not as good.'

The critic Ann Hollander has proposed that male fashion designers lean toward 'total visual effect' over the functionalist approach of female designers, which celebrates the 'working beauty of the garment in wear'. This dichotomy of 'optical' versus 'tactile' provides a useful framework for viewing Yamamoto's designs as portrayed by this notably all-male publication team. With Knight's interest in 'new ways of looking' and Saville's grave pedestals, tactility is all but subsumed, and sexuality is removed from the ceremony. As Yamamoto's clothes sought to redefine and reshape the body, the catalogues pursued increasingly fragmented modes of presentation.

Knight caught the de-sexualised aspect of Yamamoto's work from the outset. 'He was saying something different, which I felt I could adhere to. It was not a sexual approach to dressing, which most fashion had been up to that point. He was putting that in the background and presenting an intellectual form.'

Ironically, the most iconic and fêted piece to emerge from the Ascoli/Saville/ Knight collaborations is perhaps the most sexually charged. Known to Saville and Knight as the 'Suzy smoking' catalogue, the autumn/winter 1988–9 women's wear book was actually the result of a reshoot, prompted by Yamamoto's dissatisfaction with the direction in which Ascoli appeared to be steering the publicity. It includes a series of smouldering images of the model Suzy Bick, first reclining on (to the point of slipping from) a chair, beneath a plume of cigarette smoke; then positioned, in fur-lined coat and leather gloves, behind the splitting seam of a leather couch, her eye directed downward. In the following shot she appears in the same position, but looking, head half-bowed, directly at the camera. The effect of flipping the page is to cause a suggestive cinematic wink. The utter decorum in the sequence only seems to fuel its eroticism. Yet it was, according to Saville, Yamamoto's least favourite shoot.

'Suzy smoking' turned out to be the last of the collaborative catalogues. Ascoli and Yamamoto split and the next two years' publicity was produced without an art director. Saville returned to work for Yamamoto alone for the 1991–2 catalogue and a number of other publicity pieces. In many ways, these projects represent the concluding steps in the increasing abstraction of the process of depicting clothes. The 1991 menswear ad campaign, titled *Game Over* features no clothes or models at all – merely a sequence of stock images from a photo library, 'stuff that's so wrong it's right', as Saville puts it. Yamamoto's disillusionment with the fashion business, according to Saville, had coincided with a sobering recession. 'The lifestyle promise of designer clothing doesn't really make much sense in a bankrupt economy,' says Saville. The advertisements featured a series of sober, if somewhat obtuse messages. A stock image of a flower with a limp stamen, as Saville wryly notes, sits beneath the text 'This was Tomorrow', a reference to the landmark Pop Art exhibition *This is Tomorrow*. The campaign was greeted with bafflement in the fashion world. Though fashion was increasingly driven by calculated notions of lifestyle and image, no-one, it seemed, was quite ready to completely depart from the material goods being sold,

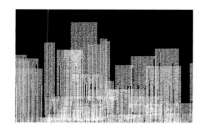

Yohji Yamamoto
Detail from six-page advertisement 1990
Art direction Peter Saville
Design Pentagram

E Z Go Printemps Eté 92 Yohji Yamamoto
Art direction Peter Saville
Photography Trevor Key

and completely divorce the signifier from the signified. That would come later. As Ted Polhemus put it in 1998, 'semiotics rather than aesthetics is the *raison d'être* of today's fashion industry'.

Saville's final catalogue for Yamamoto returned to the traditional photoshoot, only with video stills and photography by Nina Schultz, juxtaposed with more stock imagery. The theme was 'street life' with models dressed in sneakers, playing basketball under highways and clutching skateboards. The men's catalogue was incorporated within the women's, with a sequence of grainy black and white shots showing performance artist Bruce McLean dancing in three Yamamoto jackets. The eclectic result, which took many cues from contemporary artists, particularly Richard Prince, was greeted with more howls of protest. It was 'not fashion,' complained editors. Inevitably, Saville's last Yamamoto projects pre-empted an array of developments to come. Ten years later, blown out, pixellated imagery, snapshot chic, video *verité* and the mood board – filled with images vying to evoke the season's sartorial message – are part of the lexicon.

One might conclude that Saville's uncanny instinct for nailing a trend a few months or even years before its time, demonstrates that he might have fared better on the inside of the business. He admits as much: 'I was channelled into graphics by my teacher, but I probably should have done photography or fashion.' He adds, 'I was always more influenced by fashion than by any other discipline.'

As a body of work, however, the Yamamoto catalogues mark a turning point in the transformation of fashion to a cacophony of styles and modes of representation. In their own, controlled way, these projects marched through a series of experiments in divorcing fashion advertising from its duty to convey the look and feel of clothing, to the point where it becomes the play of indices.

And like the proverbial tropical butterfly that flaps its wings, setting off a tornado in another part of the world, this period of intense activity brought about a mini tempest in the world of fashion communications. They introduced a much-mimicked photographic lexicon and acquainted the fashion world with the benefits of a refined level of graphic design. The limited-edition catalogue became part of the whole fashion-publicity-editorial machine, a means by which *haute couture* could elevate itself above the increasingly segmented rabble of styles and brands. If fashion 'prescribes the ritual by which the fetish of merchandise is adored', as Walter Benjamin famously noted, the Yamamoto catalogues demonstrated that inciting that adoration is an artistic pursuit capable of hitting some sublime notes.

95

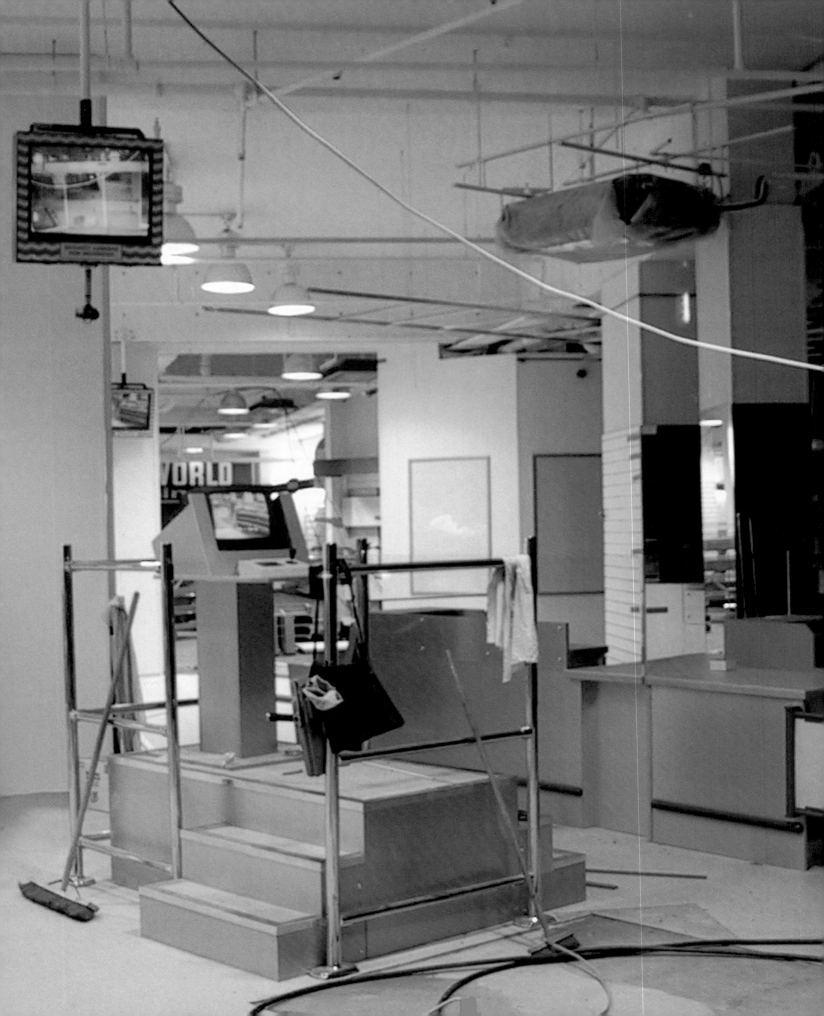

Visual merchandising

Miranda Sawyer

It might seem excessive to blame the decline of the British high street on a graphic designer from Altrincham, but you know what? I do. It's all Peter Saville's fault. It was his desire to make the everyday amazing, to bring beauty to the masses, to democratise design that led, eventually, to the state we live in today. Lifestyle UK's corporate coffee shops and you're-worth-it accessories have a history. Despite what we're told, our brand-managed living didn't spring fully formed from the loins of the American mall. It's Saville's test-tube baby.

Not that he approves. He hates, as we all do, the way that every shop, from Woolies to Gap, is exactly the same as its brothers. Quite cool, fairly pretty, sharp with a blunted edge. Just designed enough. Anathema to Saville, whose work is, and always was, nothing less than iconic. Minimal, witty, hard even when sumptuous, his clarity of vision and elegance of communication catches the eye and sears the memory. Such dazzling vision was destined to influence. Consumer companies wanted similar success, but with less effort, less thought, less outlay. So, though his work was neutered as it was nicked, these days we have Saville sewn through the fabric of our lives.

Normal life has always robbed its fringes, taken revolutionary ideas and toned them down for the consumption of all comers. Now, Saville imitations are everywhere. I've still got one of his early Haçienda posters and it could be used today. All contemporary club flyers resemble Saville's work for the Haç: he constructed the contemporary language of clubbing's graphic design. The most obvious legacy is in the branding of Cream, or Ministry of Sound, but look and you'll see it everywhere: clear, sans serif type; bright colours; no figures unless a picture of an ironic idol. Saville was also one of the first to use the ultra-photograph:

World New Order
London single 1993
Art direction Peter Saville
Design Howard Wakefield

A Little Soul Pulp
Island single 1998
Art direction John Currin and Peter Saville
Photography Horst Diekgerdes
Design Howard Wakefield
and Paul Hetherington

Play by 01/96 Various artists
London album 1995
Art direction Peter Saville
Design Howard Wakefield

those shots of natural beauty so sharp and clear they seem to vibrate before your eyes, used most famously for the sleeve of *Republic*. These days, every cool bar has a wall with an ultra-photograph on it. A desert scene in The Standard in LA; waterfalls in London's Electricity Showrooms.

For many years, Saville had the uncanny knack of knowing when a graphic style was coming up cool. The darkly glossy glamour of his work with Suede and Pulp preceded fashion's turn to gothic cocktail chic. Or how about the walking man of Gay Dad? Check out the cover of John Lanchester's *Mr Phillips* (2000) a few years later, the culmination of a trend towards information as design, transforming signage into a thing of beauty. It's as though Saville sounds the alarm, and the mainstream gives us the echo.

Of course, it wasn't just him: Ben Kelly, the interior designer Saville brought into Factory, has also been co-opted and diluted to form our current commercial and leisure environments. Before Kelly designed the Haçienda and Dry Bar, nightclubs were either dark and scuzzy, or of the glitzy Prince-video type – and bars just didn't exist. It were pub or nowt. I look at Manchester now, with its plate-glass saloons and restaurants, its urban lofts and stop-the-traffic museums, and it is physically a different city to the one of my youth. The Haçienda was the daddy of that renaissance. Cool, industrial, with an awful lot of empty space: its lines spread from the north-west to become the blueprint of today's clubs (Fabric) and bars (any drinkerie where there's a mirror behind the optics and a choice of bottled beers). And further: you can see the Haçienda in sandwich chain Prêt à Manger's flooring; it whispers through the Science Museum's airy spaces.

I remember the dark grey marble plaque outside the Haçienda with its restrained red and white typography and the Haç membership card bordered with the yellow and grey of the club's bollards. Modern adverts for modern commodities. Some of the world's most influential business people are Peter Saville fans: he was asked to do the identity for the US's educational TV program Channel One by David Neuman because Neuman was a New Order man. Fashion designer Raf Simons based two whole collections around his teenage obsession with all things Factory. These are acknowledged, direct tributes to Saville. But perhaps more amazing is the subtle shift in everyday taste that rippled out from his talent and changed our closest environments.

What Saville did was to make the ordinary (record sleeves, posters) gorgeous; he believed we should have the best. And since he did it within the surrounds of pop music, everyone's first introduction to art and the one we're most obsessive about, he hit us early and in the heart. We grew up knowing that God was in the details, that we deserved quality, because Saville and Ben Kelly and Factory had given us it from day one. Of course the high street had to wise up. Having been given the best by the edges, the centre could not hold us. The clubs are rubbish? Hold your own illegal rave. The bars are terrible? Fly to Europe. Or open your own. Brands have been forced to offer us something more: we're more sophisticated consumers, with more educated ideas about style and beauty and what a decent cup of coffee tastes like. And I blame Peter Saville for that.

There's a definition of art that says it is 'the treatment of the commonplace with the feeling of the sublime'. Today's high street treats the commonplace with a thin wash of that emotion. But underneath it all is Saville's work, and that was, as the song has it, more than a feeling. The sublime has been sublimated, but it's still sublime.

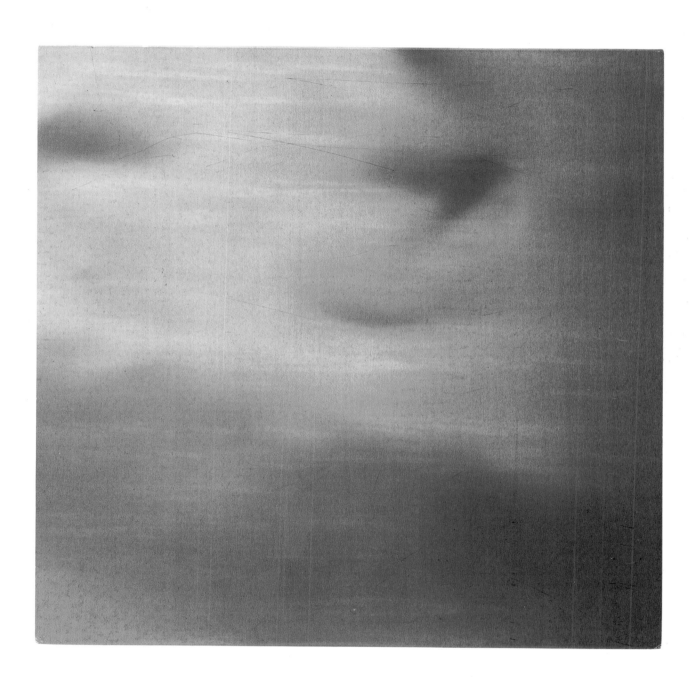

State of the Nation New Order
Factory single 1986
Photography Trevor Key
Design PSA

Brotherhood and *Bizarre Love Triangle* New Order
Factory album and single 1986
Photography Trevor Key
Design PSA

Compact
Installation 1986
White Columns Gallery, New York

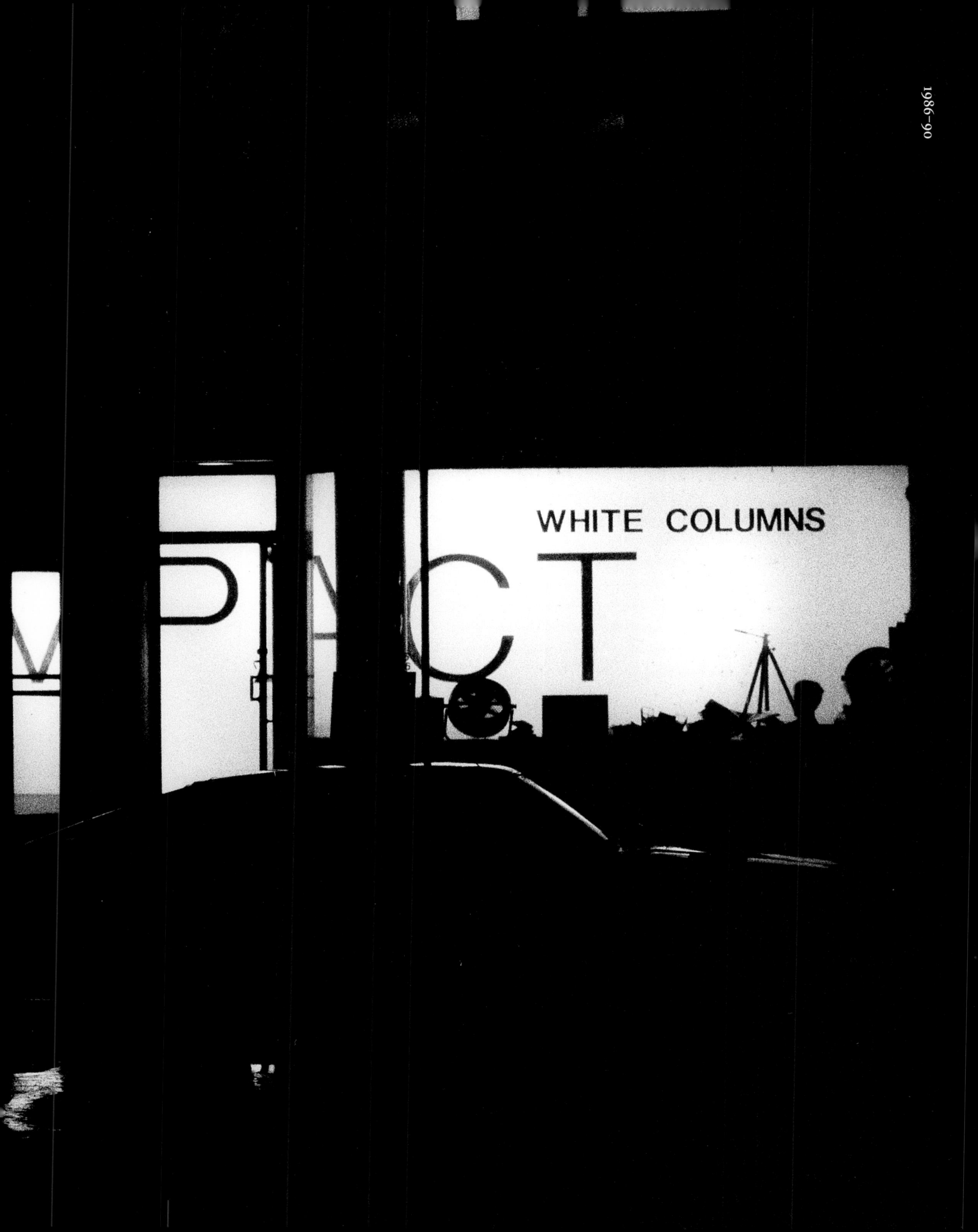
WHITE COLUMNS

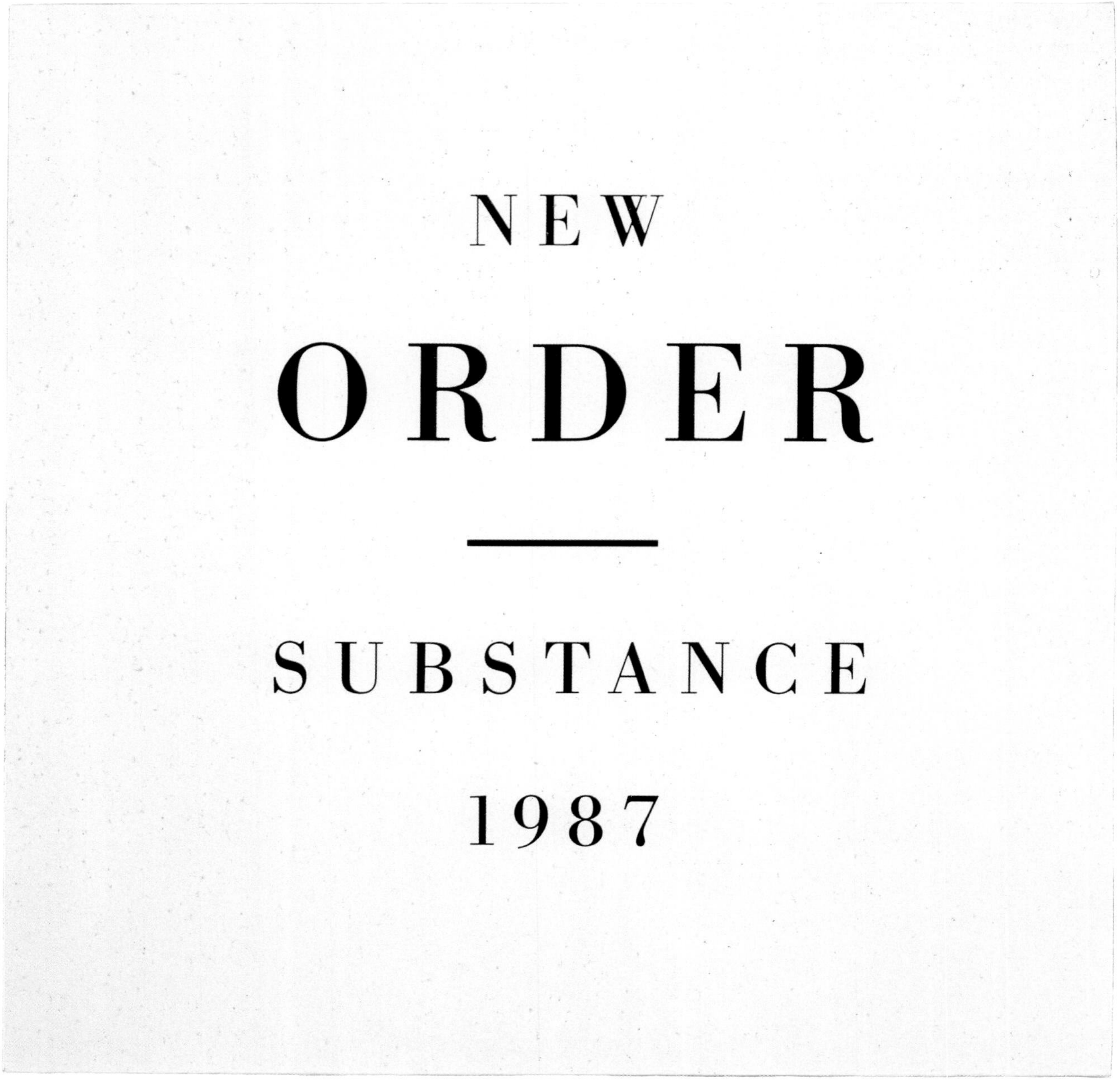

NEW
ORDER
——
SUBSTANCE
1987

Substance New Order
Factory album 1987
Design PSA

True Faith **New Order**
Factory single 1987
Dichromat Trevor Key and Peter Saville
Design PSA

Brett wickens and jah wobble 6020

Between Two Frequencies
Brett Wickens and Jah Wobble
General Kinetics single 1986
Design Brett Wickens

Blue Monday 1988 **New Order**
Dichromat Trevor Key and Peter Saville
Remastered by Howard Wakefield 2003

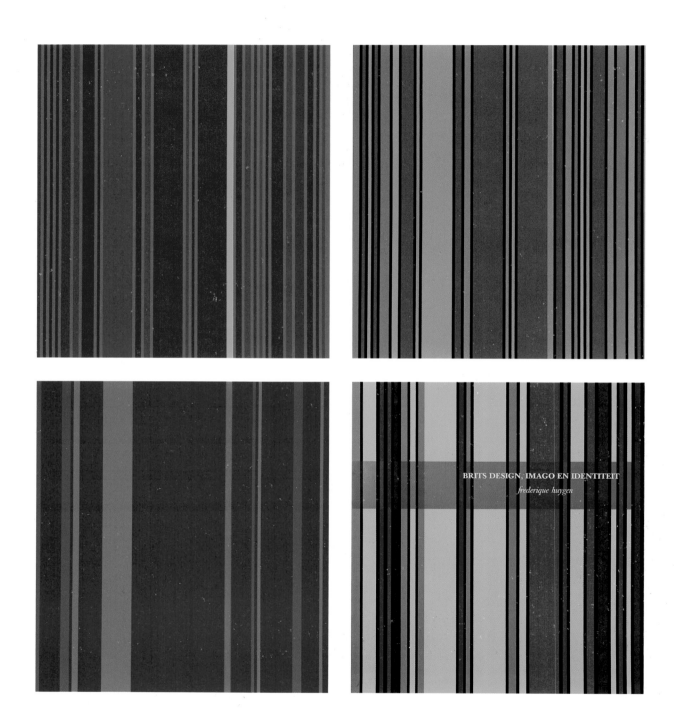

Brits Design, Imago en Identiteit Frederique Huygen
Museum Boijmans van Beuningen catalogue cover and variations 1988
Design PSA

7
Festival of the 10th Summer installation 1986
Manchester City Art Gallery
Design PSA
Construction John Harwood

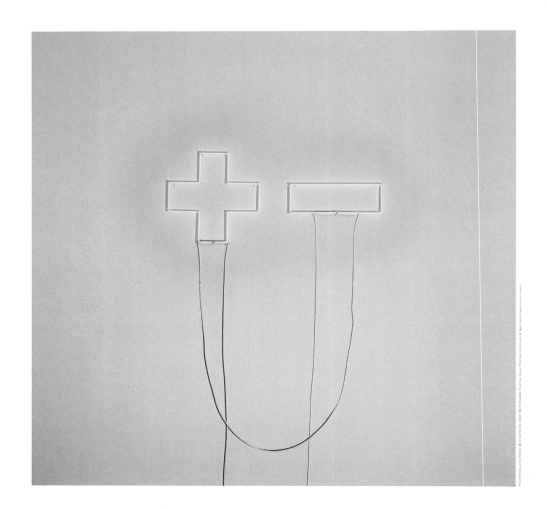

JOY DIVISION
1979
ヿ┝modヮHEre

Fac213, Fac213/7, Facd213, Facdv213.

Atmosphere and *Substance* Joy Division
Posters 20×30" 1988
Plus en Min (detail) and *Energie-Piek Ijs* (detail)
by Jan van Munster 1981
Art direction Peter Saville
Photography Trevor Key
Typography Brett Wickens

JOY DIVISION
1977-1980
bubSt7nce

Fact250, Fact250c, Facd250, Fact250d.

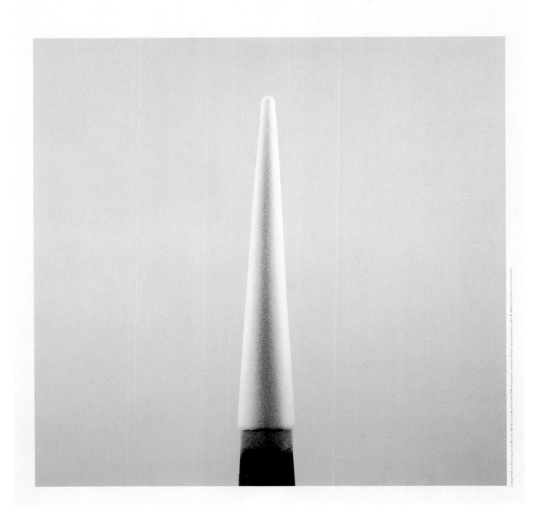

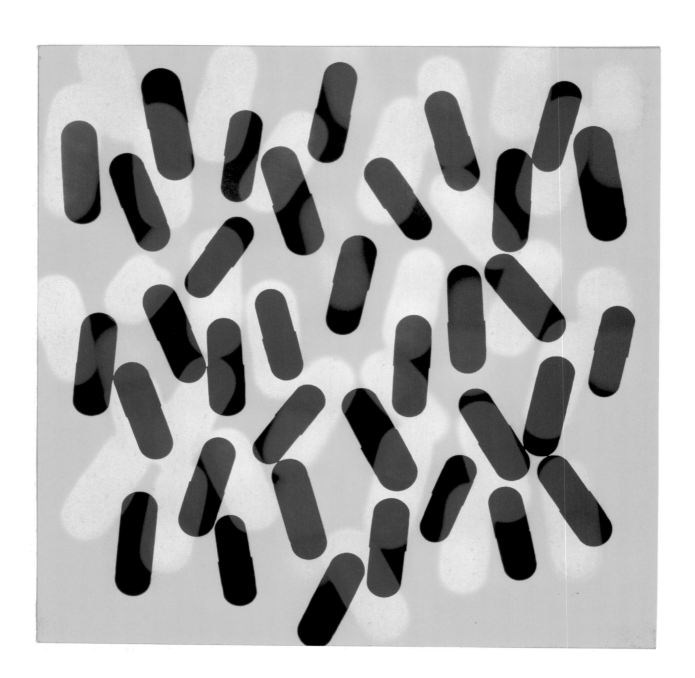

Fine Time **New Order**
Factory single 1988
Dichromat Trevor Key and Peter Saville
after a painting by Richard Bernstein
Design PSA

113

Technique New Order
Factory album 1989
Dichromat Trevor Key and Peter Saville
Design PSA

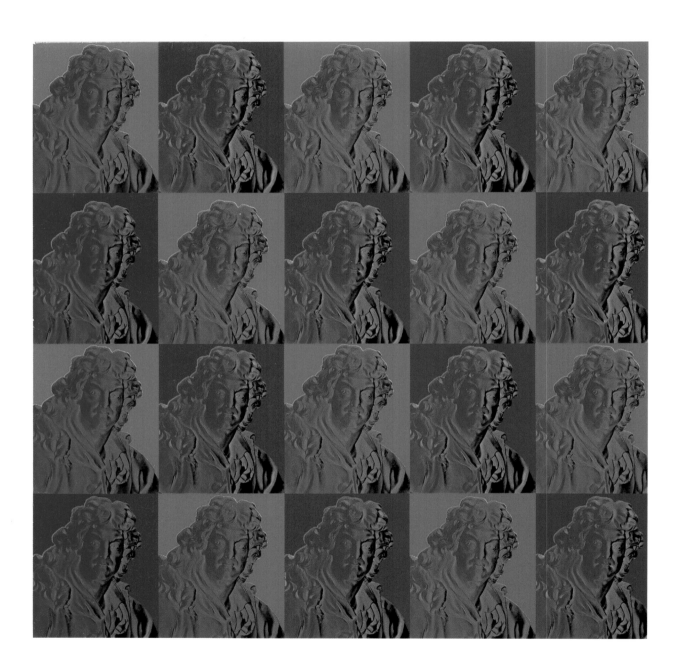

114

Round & Remix New Order
Factory single 1989
Dichromat Trevor Key and Peter Saville
Design PSA

Overleaf
Untitled New Order
Catalogue 1989
Art direction Peter Saville
Photography Donald Christie
Design PSA

USA89 New Order
T-shirt print
Design Brett Wickens

#22 ...playing hard to get still works in the 1980's

118

halluçienda

Monday Nights
DJ's + Groups, Groups + DJ's

119

Halluçienda
Poster 30 × 40" 1989
Photograph Science Photo Library
Design Julian Morey

Getting away with it Electronic
Factory single 1989
Design PSA

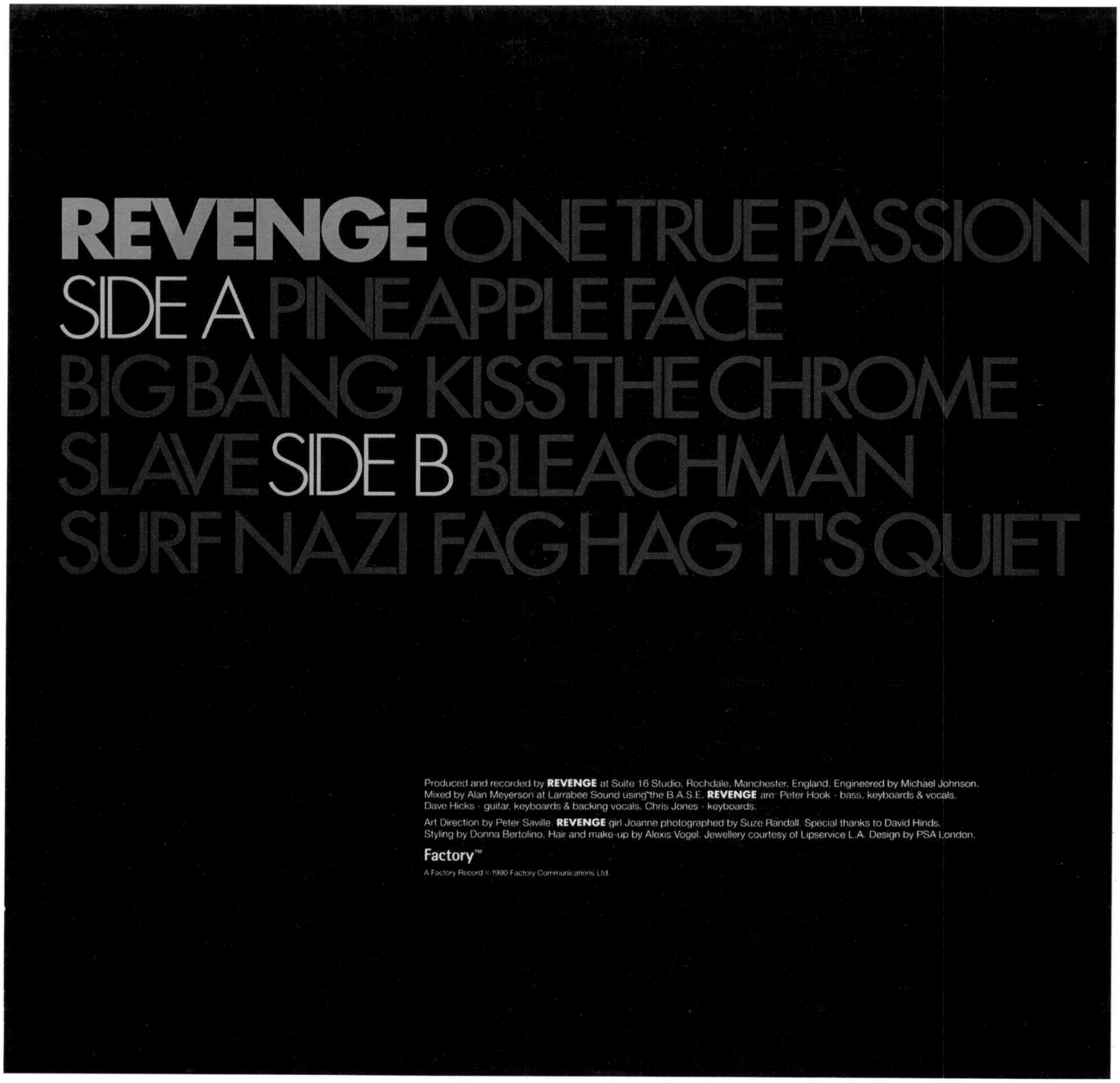

REVENGE ONE TRUE PASSION
SIDE A PINEAPPLE FACE
BIG BANG KISS THE CHROME
SLAVE SIDE B BLEACHMAN
SURF NAZI FAG HAG IT'S QUIET

Produced and recorded by **REVENGE** at Suite 16 Studio, Rochdale, Manchester, England. Engineered by Michael Johnson. Mixed by Alan Meyerson at Larrabee Sound using the B.A.S.E. **REVENGE** are: Peter Hook - bass, keyboards & vocals. Dave Hicks - guitar, keyboards & backing vocals. Chris Jones - keyboards.

Art Direction by Peter Saville. **REVENGE** girl Joanne photographed by Suze Randall. Special thanks to David Hinds. Styling by Donna Bertolino. Hair and make-up by Alexis Vogel. Jewellery courtesy of Lipservice L.A. Design by PSA London.

Factory™

A Factory Record © 1990 Factory Communications Ltd.

One True Passion Revenge
Factory album 1990
Art direction Peter Saville
Photography Suze Randall
Design PSA

Automne Hiver 91–92 Yohji Yamamoto
Art direction Peter Saville at Pentagram

123

Automne Hiver 91–92 Yohji Yamamoto
Art direction Peter Saville at Pentagram

A snow white tan

Peter York

… that's how he's always looked to me. I thought the line was written for Peter Saville, sitting in a corner downstairs at the Groucho, looking pale and waxy in a good way, with his lank black hair and stubble. He'd either be on his own – very much on his own – or with one beautiful girl at a time. Not grouping, networking, working the room; all the things I do.

You couldn't imagine – and I promise you I'm not working up to *Conversations with a Vampire* – Saville around earlier in the day or out in the sunshine. His clothes have always been good, clever with a nice little bit of observation and subtext in them, but not so as to spoil the effect. He spends real money on clothes, follows the designers – knows what they're doing. The rest of his money goes on dinner and sex. He's got his priorities right; it's really engaging.

The other thing that's engaging is his completely crazed perfectionism, his search for genuine elegance in things. It's terribly like his first pop-culture hero Bryan Ferry. Ferry who takes years to do anything, who's got this agonising fastidiousness that means he could never have been a big US stadium act – even if he'd wanted to. In last year's *24 Hour Party People* biopic about Tony Wilson and the Factory Records years there's one running joke. Saville – played to his enormous relief by someone really good-looking – comes up to the Tony Wilson character (played by Steve Coogan as Alan Partridge, it has to be said) and shows him a concert poster or a record sleeve. The poster is wonderful, the sleeve brilliant, but the concert in question is tonight, and the sleeve proves so expensive to make that there's no profit in shifting millions of New Order units.

Saville's difficult, not in any old-fashioned controversialist way, but because he really cares about the work, works himself up about it and, increasingly doesn't

Sunset Marquis 1999
Photography Peter Saville

Spring Summer 03 Stella McCartney
Advertisement
Creative direction Peter Saville
Art Direction Sascha Behrendt
and Marcus Werner Hed
Photography David Vasiljevic
Image manipulation Chris Roome at Metro

Movement Visionaire
Lenticular cover 2000
Art direction Peter Saville
Photography Nick Knight
Typography Howard Wakefield

Printemps Eté 98 Christian Dior
Campaign image
Art direction Peter Saville and Van Trahn
Photography Nick Knight

want to do the dull stuff, the throughput that the big design machines handle. 'The clients who really need you aren't good to work for; I don't want to put pen to paper for 100% banality' he says. So he's not 100% user-friendly. I love the story – apocryphal or not – that he argued with Bernard Arnault about the work he was doing for John Galliano at Dior in the mid-nineties. And got fired. Any remotely careerist designer being wanting to make it in luxury-land knows you don't argue with Arnault.

It's got all the cult elements, Saville's story. You have to start with a body of work done, with hindsight, well before its time. That elegance for the people; all those references to classical modernism, everything that seems so very late nineties now. It helps to have done your definitive work in a mythic time and place, under conditions of total anarchy. The Factory Records story couldn't be better. Madness, suicide and utter uncommercialism, a success despite itself. All the intensity of that whole crew of Mancs looking for the light.

Then you need a very gappy output, a modest output, not a predictable flow with a growing machine to back it up. Plus the nomadic personal life. Single, childless – and sometimes apparently homeless – at forty-seven. No healthcare plan. The despair of his supportive middle-class parents.

Add to this those stories which have him living with one or other prominent musical girl, here or there – of course he spent a couple of crucial years in LA – throughout the eighties and nineties. It's just perfect for a retrospective, a rediscovery.

What Peter Saville anticipated, moving from music to high fashion to art, from the late seventies on, was the trajectory of a new taste. The taste of people just a little younger than him, people, say, thirty-five through forty-two, whose opinions really matter now. Younger designers, in art school when the Factory covers were appearing, thinking this is what we want – the work and the life. And not just designers, of course, just people with a responsive eye who are running all kinds of things, a first generation of design-conscious CEOs of this and that. I see them all the time. Stable citizens, bankable types, stalwarts of New Labour and God knows what else, with the surprising houses and the unmistakable musical histories. All testimony to the idea that you don't need to reach all the people, just the ones who'll matter in the next generation. The creatures down below, as that very important disco single of 1977 *Supernature* had it, were growing up in a most peculiar way.

What they wanted, of course, was elegance on tap, the real thing from the pure sources – not eighties retro piss-elegance and not the appalling third-rateness of British everyday design of the seventies and eighties. It's amusing in retrospect, that provincial world of *The Grimleys*; fascinating when they re-create it for film and TV, but appalling for anyone with an ounce of taste or ambition at the time.

Those people are starting to be Saville clients now – the Alexander McQueen generation of made-its. It's what they always wanted, a Peter Saville cover, catalogue, logo, house style. When you look at Saville's more … prominent clients of the last decade you wonder who chose who – what process of seeking out on the client's part, and benign neglect of other potential work on Saville's part meant he ended up with Suede and Pulp, Givenchy and Dior and not … If you've been anywhere near a commercial design practice at scale you can guess the rest. I remember him telling me about an exchange with the owner of one of those practices. Saville's ambition, as he told it then, was to provoke a step-change, to make the whole high

At Tate Liverpool
Photography Sally Matheson 2001

street look better. Mr Big the designer said 'he wanted to make fish finger packs 10% better'. It was meant to put Saville in his place, assuming he'd want in soon enough to the big office, the big house and the big earn-out deal. But he never did.

Mass design's so much better now – so much sleeker, more literate, more knowing. From the mid-nineties – and certainly from 1997 on – the new mainstream modernism swept away all before it in the restaurants and the high streets and everywhere else. And you couldn't find anyone under thirty, in the most benighted burg or the worst sink estate that couldn't cite four or five designer names. Saville hates it, of course, this devoutly longed-for change 'what was once caring is now positioning – it's the blight of the last decade, so you don't want any of it … everyone knows; it's increasingly hollow'.

He's somewhere between the business of design and the business of art now – but eminently collectable. All his notebooks, the overmatter, would blow up and frame up a treat. The status of designers in art-land is a tricky thing, of course – 'I don't want to be a pretend artist, a second division runner'. Better to let them seek him out, better to let it happen on his own terms, which are arrogant, exacting and, like the man in the film, deliciously haphazard.

Happy Next Year! Yohji Yamamoto
New Year card 1992
Art direction Peter Saville at Pentagram

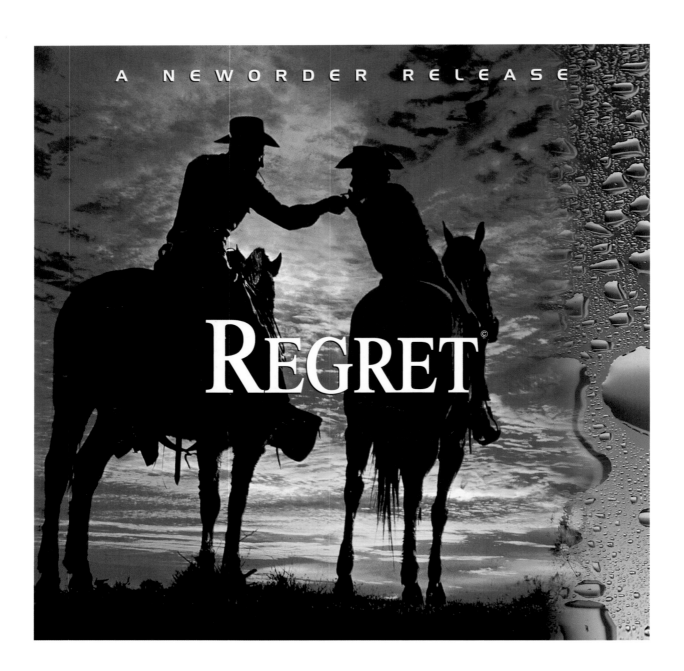

A NEWORDER RELEASE

R<small>EGRET</small>©

Regret **New Order**
London single 1993
Art direction Peter Saville
Image manipulation Brett Wickens
Designed at Pentagram

Above and overleaf
Republic New Order
London album 1993
Art direction Peter Saville
Image manipulation Brett Wickens
Designed at Pentagram

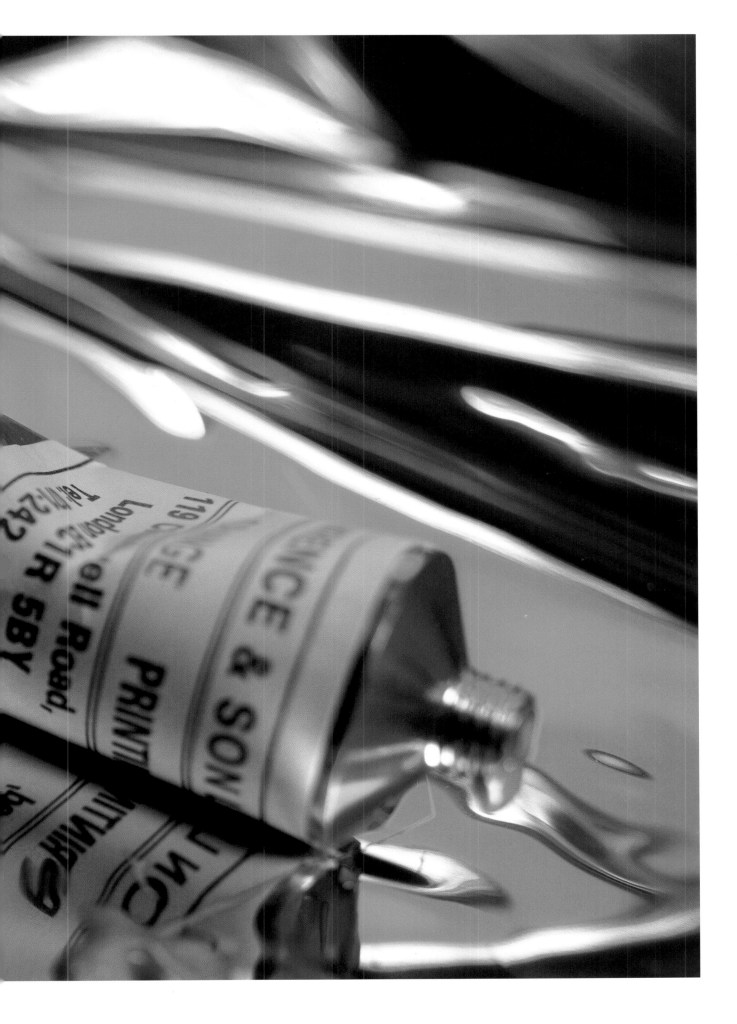

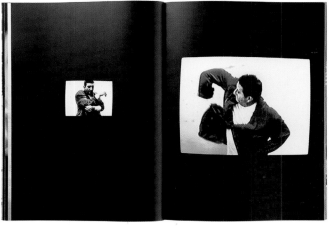

Pages 134–137
E Z Go Printemps Eté 92 Yohji Yamamoto
Art direction Peter Saville
Styling Melanie Ward
Photography Donald Christie, Trevor Key, Norbert Schoerner, Nina Schultz
Design Pentagram

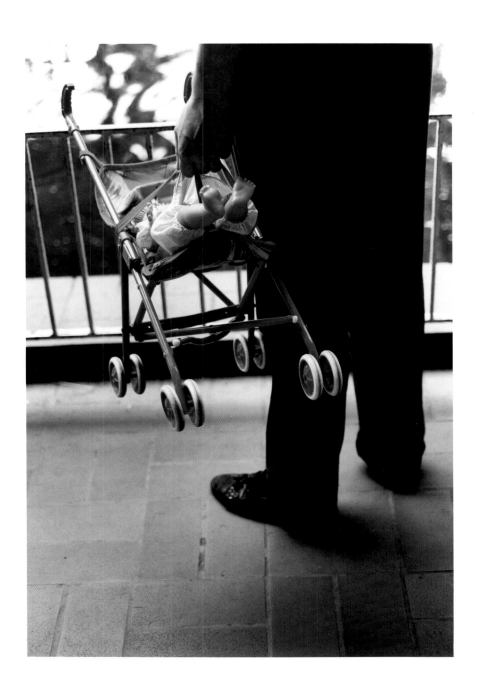

Berlin 1992
Art direction Peter Saville
Styling Melanie Ward
Photography David Sims

Santa Monica 1993
Lingerie editorial after John Kacere
Art direction Peter Saville
Photography Klaus Laubmayer

City at Night 1994
View from Las Alturas
Art direction Peter Saville
Photography Dean Chamberlayne

Blue Monday 1995 New Order
London single
Art direction Peter Saville
Design Howard Wakefield

143

(the best of) **NewOrder**

(The Best of) **New Order**
London album 1994
Design consultant Peter Saville
Design Howard Wakefield at Thomas Manss & Company
Photography Trevor Key
Digital imaging Martin Orpen at Idea

SUNRISE '94

Sunset 93 Sunrise 94 Yohji Yamamoto
New Year card
Art direction Peter Saville
Design Brett Wickens

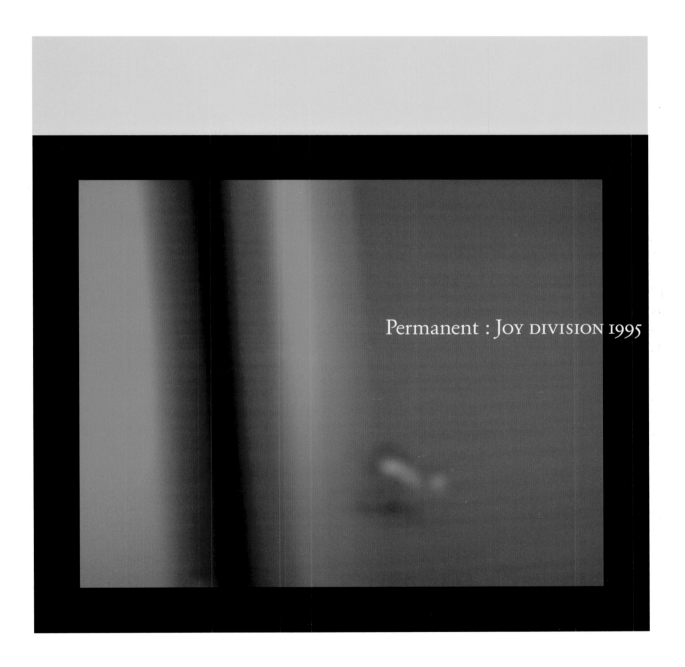

Permanent : JOY DIVISION 1995

145

Permanent Joy Division
London album 1995
Art Direction Peter Saville
Photography John Holden
Design Howard Wakefield

GUNS, DRUGS & NO MONEY

THE INTERNATIONAL AIRPORT

PICCADILLY PLAZA,
GEORGE BEST, PIGEONS

IT WAS BETTER THAN IT IS NOW

342,600

IRWELL, MEDLOCK, IRK & TIB

Manchester Records
Identity proposal 1995
Concept Peter Saville
Design Howard Wakefield

MANDARINA DUCK

147

Mandarina Duck
Logotype 1995
Art direction Peter Saville
Design Howard Wakefield

148

Flora **Nick Knight**
Schirmer Mosel Verlag 1996
Art direction Peter Saville
Design Paul Barnes and Howard Wakefield

PlantPower rubber
Natural History Museum 1992
Installation design David Chipperfield
Art direction Peter Saville
Photography Nick Knight

150

Coming Up Suede
Nude album 1996
Cover Nick Knight, Peter Saville and Brett Anderson
Paintbox Steve Seal
Design Howard Wakefield at the apartment

Filmstar Suede
Nude single 1997
Cover Nick Knight, Peter Saville and Brett Anderson
Paintbox Steve Seal
Design and post-production Howard Wakefield
at the apartment

152

This is Hardcore Pulp
Island album 1998
Art direction John Currin and Peter Saville
Photography Horst Diekgerdes
Casting Sascha Behrendt
Styling Camille Bidault-Waddington
Design Howard Wakefield and Paul Hetherington
at the apartment

Different colours, different shades

Rick Poynor

If Peter Saville's designs of the 1980s embrace the possibilities of the emerging design culture with unqualified enthusiasm, his work since the end of that decade is a protracted and increasingly troubled series of questions about the cultural position of design and the way it is used. The paradox is that he continues to be celebrated as the embodiment of a way of thinking about design that he now rejects in the strongest terms. He explains the differences between design in the 1980s and 1990s using revolution and government as a metaphor. 1980s style culture rebelled against the visual drabness of 1970s Britain and, for Saville, this was a worthwhile end in itself. This aesthetic 'revolution' succeeded and design, now in a governing position, is taken for granted by business and public alike. No commercial enterprise that hopes to achieve credibility in the contemporary marketplace can afford to ignore its power to position the product and seduce the buyer. In this respect, design's journey from fringe to mainstream is no different from the fate of so many other cultural ideas and forms of expression that began as rebellions against the norm. In *The Deviant's Advantage* (2002), American business trend-watchers Ryan Mathews and Watts Wacker exultantly trace the path by which deviant ideas move through five predictable stages, from the fringe, to the edge, to the 'realm of the cool', to the next big thing, until finally they turn into conventions accepted by everyone. At this point they are ready to become mass markets. The conclusion for smart entrepreneurs: look to the fringe. The relatively innocent design gestures of the early 1980s, when the mechanics of assimilation had yet to be tracked and exploited so ruthlessly, are simply not possible any more.

Saville's change of heart, his growing disillusion with what design had become, was prompted by experiences of personal failure that came as a shock to the system.

A day at WDR 2002
Photography Peter Saville

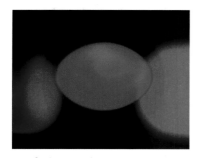

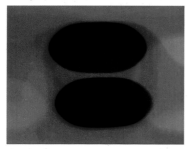

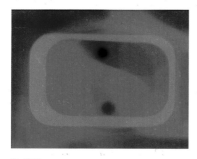

De Tijd
Film to accompany music by Louis Andriessen
Barbican Centre, London 1999
Animation Sam Roberts
Post-production The Mill

1 Bulldogge, 1 Spartakistin + 1 Berufsmodell
Paul Wunderlich
Oil on Canvas 1972

In 1991, his *Game Over* and *This was Tomorrow* ads for Yohji Yamamoto caught the mood of global recession, after this own company, Peter Saville Associates, had crashed. Influenced by the work of Richard Prince and Barbara Kruger, Saville found a perversely hallucinogenic brand of beauty in images of exhaustion and depletion. The game might be over, but one could still melt down or expire in style. In 1993, he used a similar compositional method in his *Republic* and *Regret* covers for New Order, subversively manipulating the visual codes of the entertainment industry and commercialised mass culture for the first time. Tranforming the records' titles into copylines of his own, Saville parodies the hyperreal photography and square-jawed typographic mannerisms of Hollywood billboards and film titles. Even the group's name is subsumed into the concept: A NEW ORDER RELEASE. These covers were produced at a time when most design regarded as experimental or progressive dazzled the viewer with fractured image networks and intricate webs of aberrant typographic matter. Misled by the visual simplicity of Saville's work, it was easy to overlook its conceptual and contextual sophistication. They were the last projects for New Order in which Saville was given the kind of autonomy he had enjoyed in the 1980s and they confirm that he is at his most incisive when he is allowed to pursue his own inclinations. His problem, from then on, would be to find clients who, as he puts it himself, 'have what I do as a brief'.

Even in Saville's most fully realised projects of the last decade some kind of compromise has usually been necessary. Yet despite the need to collaborate (as most design jobs require) certain themes and concerns recur. The New Order covers are based on photo library stock shots, but the smooth transitions between images were achieved using the Paintbox computer graphics system. Since then, Saville has repeatedly employed digital tools – more recently Photoshop – to manipulate various types of source image. His designs often begin with an art reference and, in the case of Suede's album *Coming Up* (1996), it was a series of symbolist and surrealist gouaches by the German artist Paul Wunderlich, painted in the 1960s and 1970s. Saville showed Wunderlich's pictures – based on nude figure studies by the photographer Karin Székessy – to Suede's Brett Anderson, and to photographer Nick Knight, who were both enthusiastic about the decadent mood they suggested. Saville was familiar with Suede's previous album, *Dog Man Star*, and preferred to act as facilitator, allowing Anderson to play the part of creative director. The androgynous image of a boy, a girl and someone who could be either was built up using Paintbox from a series of digital layers, allowing areas and details to be treated in different ways – as colour, as black and white, as solarised black and white, as colour negative, and so on. *Coming Up* is a fluently crafted blend of concrete detail and ambiguous abstraction. Where exactly is this scene happening? The sort of bare mattress one might see on a squat floor appears to float without support in a void. It's like a mind-bending scene from *Performance* restaged for the digital generation, a stylish new angle on an otherwise routine trinity: sex, drugs and rock and roll.

On Saville's cover with John Currin for Pulp's *This is Hardcore* (1998) the sense of ambiguous unease in the image is even more acute. Some concluded, taking their cue from the title stamped across the centre of the picture, like a moralistic commentary, that the naked model face down on the leather cushion had been violated, that she was meant to be dead. The contrast of mood with the 1970s Roxy Music album covers – one of Saville's early inspirations – could not be more telling.

Soft Bernard
Digital experiment 2001
Peter Saville, Howard Wakefield
and Paul Hetherington

3 16 New Order
DVD cover 2001
Peter Saville and Howard Wakefield

Sister Honey
From *Dazed & Confused: Inside Out* 2000
Art direction Peter Saville
Photography Nick Knight
Graphic art Paul Hetherington
and Howard Wakefield

The animation of those obliging fantasy figures, promising a world of unlimited satisfaction and glamour, here becomes inertia, as the woman turns inward, refusing or perhaps unable to return the viewer's voyeuristic gaze.

Saville, too, has tended to turn inwards. Much of his time now is spent reflecting and writing in his notebooks. He is interested in technology's potential to provide new visual codes and his designs aspire to represent alternative versions of reality. In recent years, much of his output has seemed to resist specificity of outline and solidity of form. Images are filtered, blurred, transmuted, remade. In projects such as the soft metallic Channel One idents (1992) and the wavering question mark cover for New Order (1994) objects were already becoming molten and malleable. Joy Division's *Permanent* compilation (1995) presents a highly contingent-looking photograph of green liquid nothingness enclosed in a heavy black frame offset by a burst of brilliant yellow. It was Photoshop, however, that allowed Saville to embrace abstract image-making, though always with its possibilities as signifier of the contemporary moment in mind. In 1998, after observing his assistant, Howard Wakefield, exploring the effects of a Photoshop filter called Wave, Saville initiated a series of collaborative Waste Paintings, using imagery the studio had been working on during the day. The filter scatters the pixels that compose the image in all directions and these shifting colour fields can be developed and refined by changing colour combinations, degrees of opacity in the image and other factors. Their surfaces melt, collapse and rush past in a seductive blur. For Saville, the Waste Paintings were a metaphor for impermanence and the speed of contemporary consumption; sampling, reprocessing and recycling these evanescent images gave them a second life and an odd kind of gravitas, too. He saw the process as a graphic version of Jane Atfield's Made of Waste furniture fashioned from tiny fragments of recycled plastic. In formal terms, the digital paintings resemble Morris Louis's canvases of the late 1950s, where veils of brilliant acrylic paint cascade down the picture plane. In art history, Pop challenged and deposed Abstract Expressionism. Saville, developing in reverse, has evolved from the Pop-derived sensibility of his early work into his own version of post-painterly abstraction. A 1998 poster for the Barbican represents American experimental music with a subliminal stars and stripes that is simultaneously discordant and exquisite.

In 1999, for Suede's *Head Music* album, the studio's focus switched from Wave to Photoshop's Median filter, which averages out areas of tonality within a digital image. The forms of the two headphone-clad figures, photographed by Nick Knight, are recognisably human, but identifying details disappear as their body contours melt into a single mass. Saville and Knight took the erotic possibilities of this kind of image a step further in a series of six pictures created for *Dazed & Confused* magazine's *Inside Out* book (2000). Saville's starting point was the voluptuous, cartoon-like fleshiness he had observed in a book of erotic oil paintings by the French artist Paul Laurenzi. Knight's 10×8-inch Polaroids of large, curvaceous women were scanned into the computer at the shoot, then manipulated in post-production, using Median, to give new meaning to the word 'softcore'. The *Sister Honey* sequence, as Saville titled it, depicts an almost suffocatingly intense universe of sensation, where objects and space fold into each other, the boundaries between bodies dissolve, flesh flows together and the self is erased.

Saville's output has slowed since the 1980s. Long experience of trying to design for clients has equipped him with persuasive arguments for not designing at all.

157

ABC Television
Proposal for development
of Paul Rand's 1962 logotype 1996
Art direction Peter Saville
Typography Paul Barnes

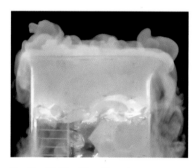

You Can Fly The Other Two
Image for London single 1999
Art direction Peter Saville
Image manipulation Howard Wakefield

He faces a genuine dilemma, which others have also described. Design has become every bit as manipulative as he declares it to be. Its global economic success means that it has turned into something less idealistic, more instrumental, and too often, as he says, what it is used to express is untrue. As a young designer, Saville was inspired by a moment of rebellion. As he is the first to acknowledge, he is temperamentally unsuited for design's 'government' role and he realised long ago that the messages that matter to him most are not the client's, but his own. There has been plenty of discussion in recent years among graphic designers about the degree to which a designer might exploit a commercial client as the unwitting channel for his or her own point of view. Saville is uncomfortable with the idea of using design in this way, despite his experience with Factory. The label was not unique in its elevation of design, but it was certainly unusual. Most companies do not value design as an end in itself; they use it for a purpose. When Saville works on identities for organisations such as Mandarina Duck or Givenchy, he tends to accept that these are the terms of the arrangement. The incremental improvements he made for each company are textbook examples of sensitive, responsible design that puts the client's needs before any personal considerations. One might ask why he doesn't push harder, but in cases where he has done this, including Mandarina Duck, he has quickly learned where the limits lie, reinforcing his view that the possibilities for design as self-expression are restricted.

So is Saville's most personal work some kind of special case, or fluke? It was created within the framework of design, but according to the designer himself, his most innovative pieces are not really design at all. From the beginning, Saville made constant references to art, borrowing from it freely as required. It's hard to think of any other designer who has done this so consistently, or with such a command of art's stylistic nuances and value as a 'code'. Is his work, in that case, art masquerading as design? To conclude that it is would be to ignore all the factors and attributes that it has in common with other designed objects. It was created for mass production and is delivered, not as a costly one-off or a limited edition, but as multiple printed copies, widely available for a modest price. What Saville's innovations suggest, above all, is the needless restrictiveness of conventional definitions of what 'art' and 'design' are supposed to be. He has developed a type of communication that combines aspects of the two practices. His work offers a prescient glimpse of the direction that hybrid forms of media might take in years to come, when circumstances allow this to happen.

Waste painting #1 1998
Paul Hetherington, Peter Saville and Howard Wakefield
Collection Emmanuel de Buretel

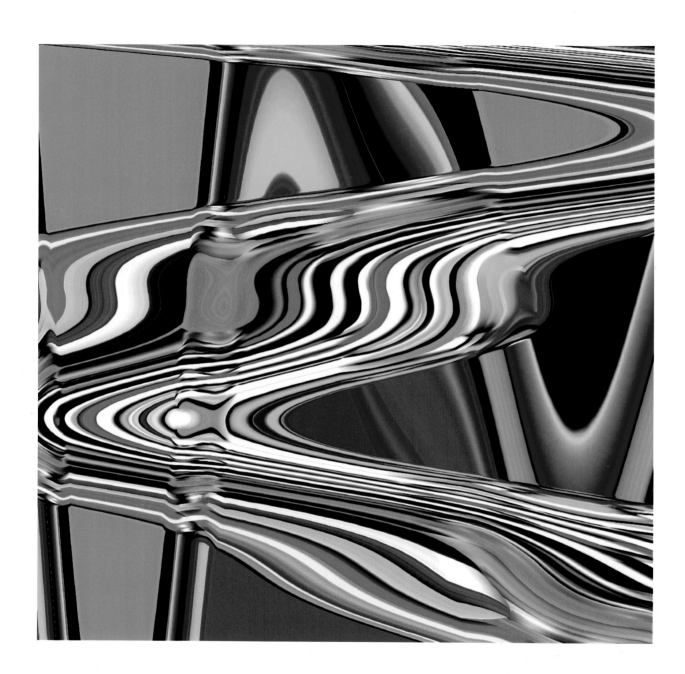

160

EMI Series
Waste Painting 2003
Peter Saville and Howard Wakefield

American Pioneers
Barbican Art Centre poster 1998
Art direction Peter Saville
Graphic art and design Paul Hetherington

Philip Glass, John Cage, Tan Dun,
La Monte Young, Steve Reich,
John Adams, Terry Riley with Pulp,
Harry Partch & Elliott Carter
American pioneers.
Innovators, rule breakers & iconoclasts

★ A Year of American Culture
INVENTING
AMERICA

Barbican Centre 23 October - 28 November
Box Office 0171 638 8891 (9am-8pm daily)

162

Electricity and *Head Music* Suede
Nude single and image for album 1999
Nick Knight, Peter Saville and Brett Anderson
Design and graphic art Howard Wakefield
and Paul Hetherington at Commercial Art

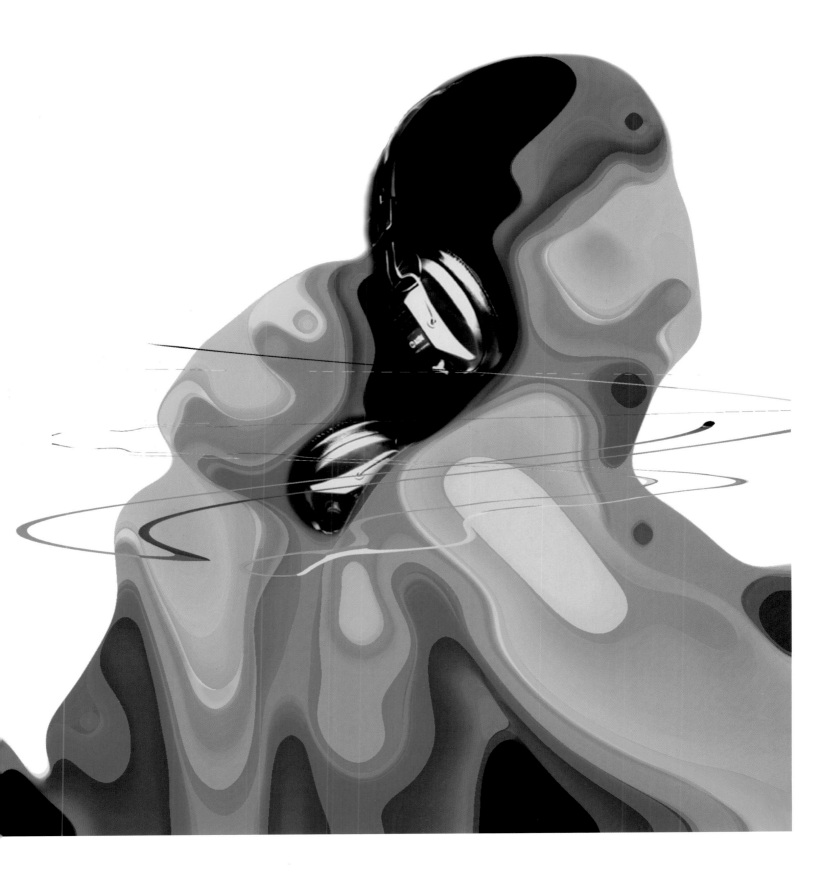

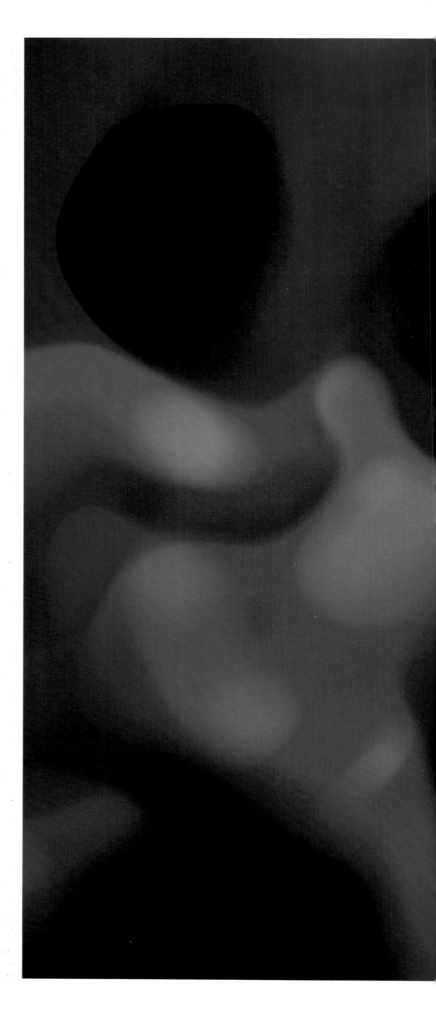

Sister Honey
From *Dazed & Confused: Inside Out* 2000
Art direction Peter Saville
Photography Nick Knight
Graphic art Paul Hetherington
and Howard Wakefield

164

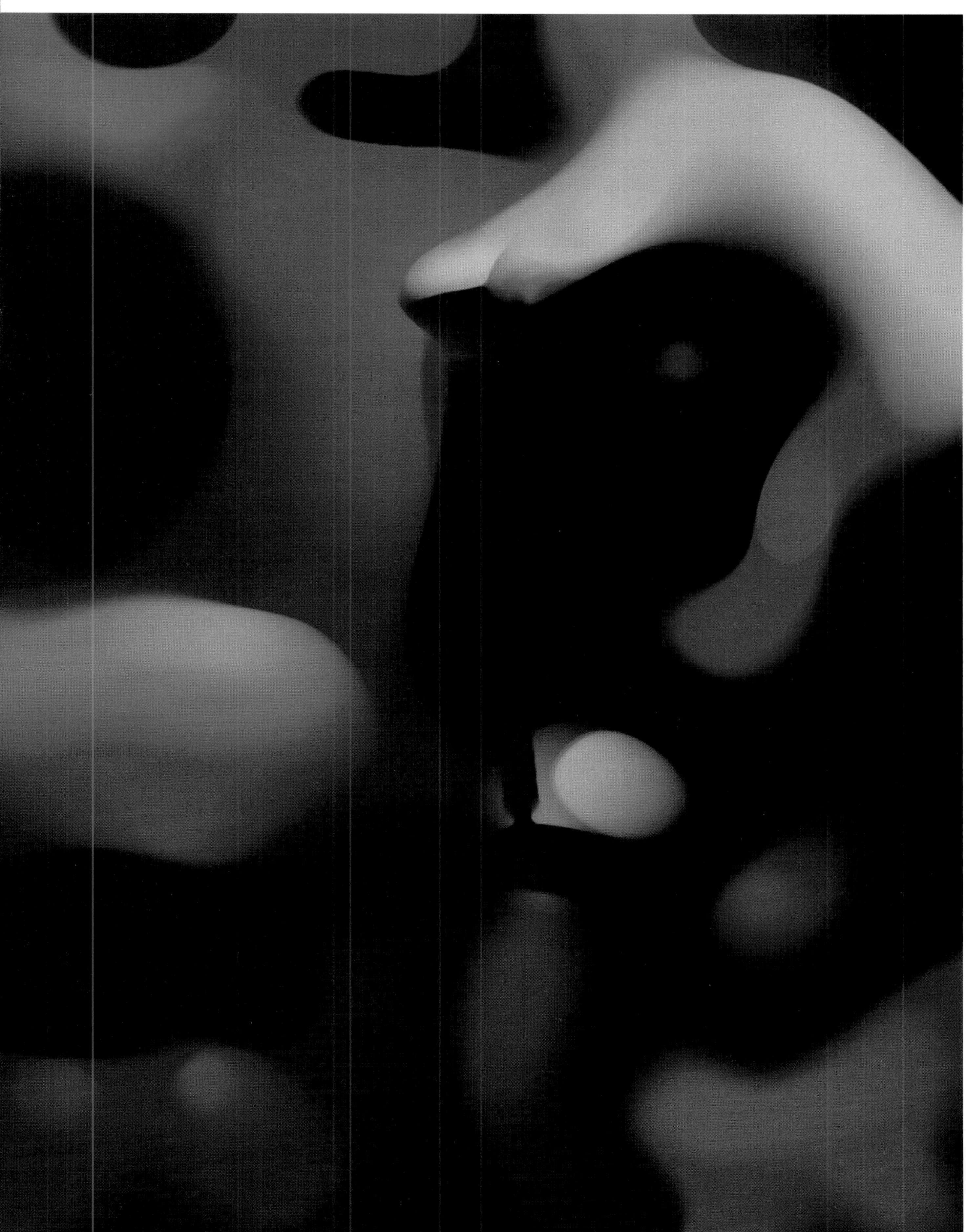

Joy! Gay Dad
Image from London single 1999
Art direction Peter Saville
Graphic art Paul Hetherington and Howard Wakefield
Designed at Commercial Art

167

Leisure Noise Gay Dad
Image from London album 1999
Art direction Peter Saville
Graphic art Paul Hetherington and Howard Wakefield
Logo concept Paul Barnes
Designed at Commercial Art

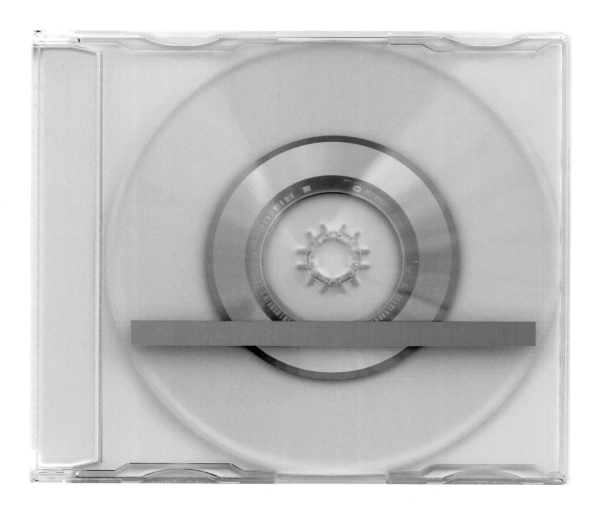

Crystal **New Order**
Proposal for London single 2001
Rendering Bill Holding at Morph UK

60 Miles an Hour **New Order**
Image for London single 2001
Art direction Peter Saville
Photography Juergen Teller
With thanks to Coco

Heart and Soul Joy Division
Image from London boxed set 1998
Art direction Peter Saville
Video still Jon Wozencroft

Retro **New Order**
Cover image from London boxed set 2002
Inspired by Helmut Lang
Art direction Peter Saville
Photography Nick Knight

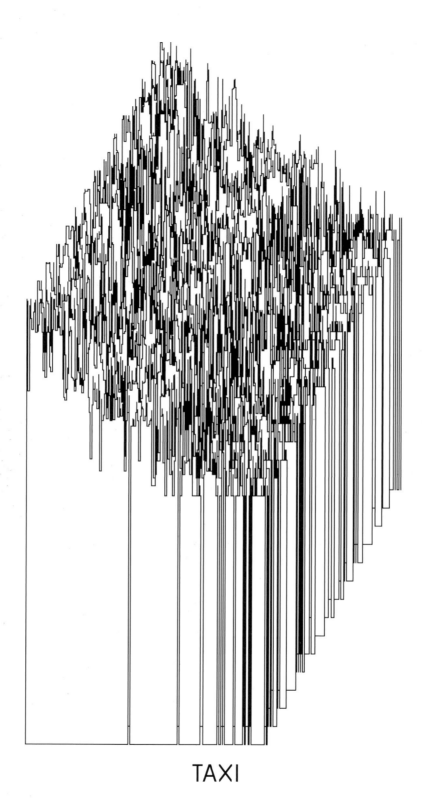

TAXI

Soundgraph – Taxi
Silkscreen on aluminium 2000
Julian Morey and Peter Saville
Collection London Records

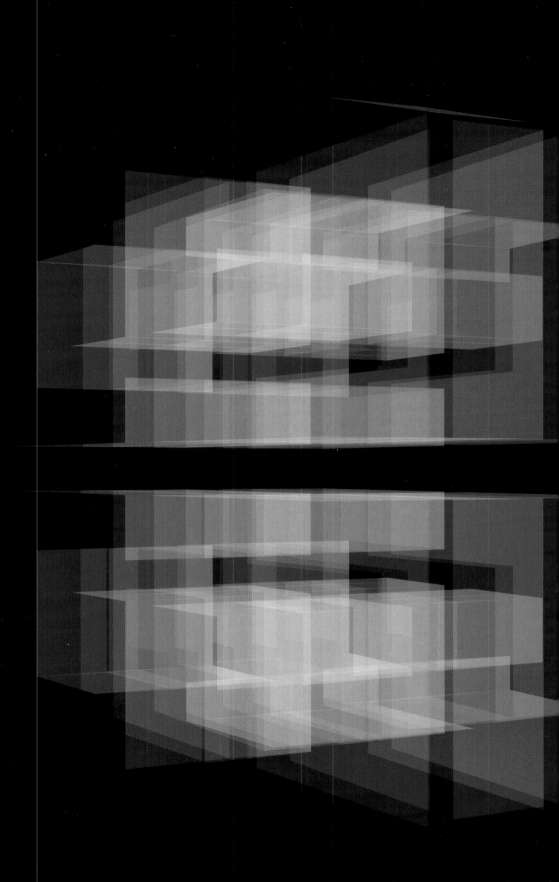

Givenchy
Digital animation 2001
Marcus Werner Hed

SHOWstudio   LILAC Peter Saville/Autechre
Audio | Info | Close

Lilac
showstudio graphic/audio project 2001
Concept and narration Peter Saville
Audio remix Autechre
Design Paul Hetherington and Derek Michael

Forget-Me-Not
showstudio interactive illustration 2001
Concept Peter Saville
Illustration Julie Verhoeven
Design Paul Hetherington

AFTER AFTER
**MONARCH OF THE GLEN
BY SIR EDWIN LANDSEER**
BY SIR PETER BLAKE
PETER SAVILLE 2002

176

177

After 'After "Monarch of the Glen"
by Sir Edwin Landseer' by Sir Peter Blake
Iris print 34 × 46" 2002
Edition of 25

Pulp logotype
Typeface by Louis John Pouchée c.1820
Art direction Jarvis Cocker and Peter Saville

178

Berlin
Viva Plus title sequence 2000
Art direction Peter Saville
Video Daniel Josefsohn and Niklas Weise

The romance of [the other end of] the telescope

Christopher Wilson

Summer 2001: Peter Saville has no home. His belongings are divided between three concrete storage cubes in Old Street and another in Wembley. Aside from these, there were some boxes upstairs at Ironmonger Row, in the empty space which was to become his new studio. No-one knew any longer what the boxes contained. Would I be interested in finding out?

I was to file and sort. Completed works, and their attendant films and artwork, were to join their filed-and-ledgered brothers in storage. I would throw out anything which I deemed worthless, and present a digestible, sifted selection of the remainder back to Saville. The work would have 'an academic aspect and a shelf-stacking aspect.' Lurking somewhere in this brief was an ulterior project motive: Saville had begun to realise the value of his own history. And while he might not wish to keep all of the contents of this heap, some of his now-grown-up 'appreciation society' would want to buy it. Like many Saville schemes, the concept was ever in a state of flux, but the basic plan was to take a boxful of archive highlights – press cuttings, printouts, rejected versions of old work – and create a screenprinted facsimile 'in a hundred copies, and we'll sell them for a thousand each'. Leaning over the restaurant table, he asked 'Wouldn't you want to buy Andy Warhol's box?' The idea was rooted in a particularly Saville kind of despair: still faced with frustration at the lack of a post-Factory 'autonomous zone' in which to function, and with the shadow of potential bankruptcy stalking his every move, he was now imagining one strand of his future built from the debris of his past. I filed and sorted.

A certain silence hangs over Saville's oeuvre, and to find oneself surrounded by the notes and sketchbooks which led to it is disconcerting. But where work is concerned, there are no direct answers here. In a typical early note, a stack of processes and art world figures audition for appropriation:

Sascha 2000
Photography Peter Saville

Sketches for the first Factory poster 1978

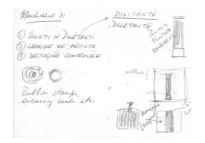

Sketchbook 1981

182

Peter Saville with Andy McCluskey
and Paul Humphreys of OMD 1981

'22/1/82.
<u>Ideas General</u>
Sound proof perforations.
Picabia + machinery
AEG + industrial technology.
Ceramics (Karme?)
Girls in industry photography.
DUCE DUCE Flags.
Architecture Fascista. (FUTURISM)
Painting.
Picasso.
Model Making.
Constructions.
Embroidery.
Europa.
Schwitters collage.
(relating to new order – emery. mesh
Martha related   etc.'[1]

Like all the hundreds of lists I found, this is transparently the work of a fashion designer. It collects whatever might encapsulate the present. But '*Ideas* General'? There are no ideas as such; only looks awaiting a suitable client, and the half-bracketed footnote seems an afterthought – perhaps some of these moods could be fixed to a current commission. By 1988 such token concessions to real work are fading. As often, Saville addresses himself in the second person:

'you are no longer very interested in your commissioned work –
what are you motivated about?
consider:
max bill
bert stern
a. warhol
fashion
glamour
sex/eroticism
image
visual things
reference
lifestyles
tech – art – pop
glamour [*sic*]
* Rosenquist
(a chromium plated dream-world)'

By January 1990 the mood has changed again. Saville looks to language as a way out, as if images could not carry ideas, and questions his 'philosophy of the moment' approach:

'Sadly, the philosophy is often "only visual" – overly narcissistic in its interest and "awareness of itself". The way you work with material can be functionalistic + purposeful in a minimal way but too often the subject matter fails to extend beyond the "image" of things – you should propose the socio-cultural links + implications of concepts more. (nb. jeff koons/nihilism of the Pet Shop Boys etc.)

'think more, reach more – don't be afraid, don't bury attitude under surface – use words?'

Wordplays are ubiquitous. The whole Saville ethos is condensed into a shift from noun to verb: 'Peter Saville associates … himself with …'. And sometimes there are blunt reminders of his view of music as just another facet of culture, another type of product. A primitive experiment in oxymorons has him grouping the phrase JOY DIVISION with the name of sanitaryware manufacturer IDEAL STANDARD!

Then there are the drawings and rough visuals. For someone associated with calculated positioning, Saville's early years were surprisingly hands-on. Although based on a Tschichold publicity leaflet cover from 1928, the first Factory poster eats a whole notebook by itself: Letraset experiments, collages, endless layout reconfigurations. Saville is 'always at some point on a scale' between classicism and modernism, and his love of this juxtaposition means that a sketch of an antique cabinet (dimensions included) may well pop up in the middle of some Ultravox roughs.

Colour codes for the Fruitmarket Gallery and New Order's 1983 releases are obsessively worked out on graph paper in coloured pencil. In counterpoint to this handmade techno, the Saville equivalent of drawing from nature is demonstrated by a sheet bearing four rows of Pantone colour-matching swatches, and over them the touching typewritten caption 'Rhodedendrons [*sic*], Holland Park 30.05.87'.

The pile I marked 'Correspondence' included everything from irate letters from clients to students requesting dissertation help. A set of fantasies faxed to the apartment by the mysterious 'K' seem designed to appeal to Saville's tastes on more than a sexual level, these little outbursts having been set in neat clusters of Helvetica.

The division between letters and work disintegrates in one case. Saville claims that the swansong of his appropriating habit came in 1984 with *Thieves Like Us*, but the true date of this *fin de siècle* would appear, when faced with letters from Suede's Brett Anderson, to be as late as 1996. Rather than choose a suitable typeface for the *Coming Up* campaign, Saville took the (selfconsciously?) eccentric scrawl in which Anderson had written him: 'By the way, our new thoughts for the cover are spot on. THINK LAZY/TRASH'. The choice was perfect for the band's starstruck romanticism, and also marks the belated logical endgame of Saville's rehashing of found elements. Where before he would have found a suitable look to give to the client, here that suitable look was the client himself: Suede sold back to Suede. 'Keep it in your pants' ends Anderson's letter, hopefully.

There were few finished works in the room, but it was a graveyard to some delicious what-ifs. *Still*'s cover was originally to be based on that of a Czech classical record, its large gold type and red background gaudy beside the final grey solution. Elsewhere, though, the rejected sketch was more intriguing than the realisation. A polaroid for *This is Hardcore* shows Pulp's Steve Mackey conversing with an older gentleman in a golf club. Saville found this a more suggestively interesting option than the chosen cover girl, and tuts when recalling that Mackey ended up with 'the most macho portrait of the lot'. The liquid question mark announcing *(The Best of) New Order* was intended to fluctuate between formats, but this was rejected as insufficiently recognisable, and Trevor Key's rippling photo sequence was entombed here.

Other also-rans did not make it into any material form, and exist only as written ideas. Although New Order's *Substance* compilation would eventually have an entirely distinct design to its Joy Division namesake, March 1987 found Saville toying with 'a "generic" logotype for the series based on the gloopy old Solidarity logo.

Letter from Brett Anderson 1996

Original reference for *Still*
See p.65

This is Hardcore Pulp
Unused shot from photo session 1998
Photography Horst Diekgerdes

183

184

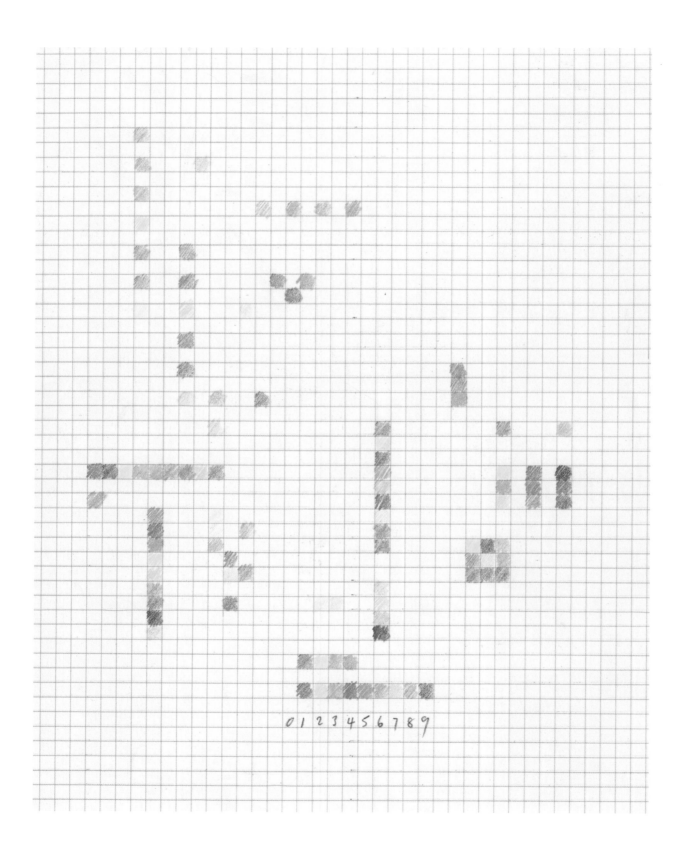

0 1 2 3 4 5 6 7 8 9

Colour code notes 1983

Rhodedendrons, Holland Park 30.05.87

PANTONE 130C · PANTONE® 134C · PANTONE® 136C · PANTONE® 137C · PANTONE 144C · PANTONE 148C · PANTONE 149C · PANTONE 151C

PANTONE 158C · PANTONE 172C · PANTONE 179C · PANTONE® 180C

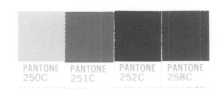

PANTONE 250C · PANTONE 251C · PANTONE 252C · PANTONE 258C

PANTONE 357C · PANTONE 364C · PANTONE 370C · PANTONE 383C · PANTONE 553C · PANTONE® 555C · PANTONE® 556C · PANTONE 576C · PANTONE 577C

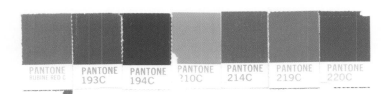

PANTONE RUBINE RED C · PANTONE 193C · PANTONE 194C · PANTONE 210C · PANTONE 214C · PANTONE 219C · PANTONE 220C

Colour study 1987

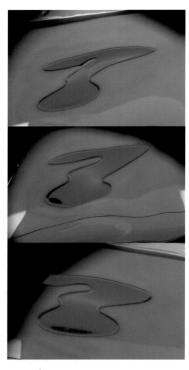

Images for *(The Best of) New Order* 1994
Photography Trevor Key

True Faith leaf 1987

Folders from PSA's Kensal Road period collate generic references by theme. The 'Industry (modern/technological)' file includes chemical hazard symbols and a Department of the Environment leaflet on *Noise control on building sites* – its cover workman obviously traced back to front for *A Factory Sample*.

Questions of found creativity and appropriation were sometimes answered. Joy Division's posthumous 1988 releases may feature the sculptures of Jan van Munster, but when the same sculptures appear in some decidedly unpromising gallery test shots, their presentation on the sleeves of *Atmosphere* and *Substance* seem far removed from Saville's early method of 'taking the paint straight from the tube'.

A similar discipline underlies the editing of imagery for *Republic* and *Game Over*, although the similarities between the stock library shots present a headache to the would-be archivist. Here Saville's listing habit at last finds commercial application: *Republic*'s picture categories included 'Side order of facts', 'Ohio Players', 'Pacific Coast Highway' and 'Logo Land'. Banal-nightmarish images of galleons, stalagmites and power stations, alongside *Amityville* lettering and, jarringly, cartoons lost out to the beach couple and their burning shack.

New Order covers have always been a canvas for Saville's current obsession, and it isn't surprising that the circumstances of his own life have sometimes strayed into the picture. With *True Faith* the eclipse is complete. Sitting behind the wheel of his parked car, recently heartbroken, he glanced up to see a leaf separate from its branch and drift down to frame itself against the windscreen. As he told me in 2001, 'That's the one piece I could sign "All my own work."' But even in such a personal case, his need for poised detachment would not rest. Anyone else might have shot *this* particular leaf, but Saville rejected it in favour of a Düreresque hunt around Windsor Great Park with Trevor Key. So my surprise at finding a shoebox containing the preserved item was tempered by slight disappointment: this perfect specimen is an impostor.

Something called 'Ephemera' slipped between my filing categories. It was a weak label, as certain motifs repeated too frequently to be passed off as random junk. Here was a plastic mermaid doll broken in half. A little later, here was a wooden mermaid with string-pull-powered parts. But their mother project was nowhere in sight.

Another recurring motif was easier to explain. When visiting his mother in Conway, north Wales, Saville often performs an absent-minded ritual in the tourist shop of neighbouring Portmerion, where cult sixties TV series *The Prisoner* was filmed. Thus I found badges bearing *Prisoner* slogans stuffed into many of the boxes, and inevitably these began to read like desperate statements about his identity crisis in the contemporary design scene: 'I am not a number I am a free man'.[2]

By now, the mission had rendered itself impossible. These badges, this endless LA hotel bill – this *is* the work, and to throw any of it away might be to nip some future 'spirit of the times' in the bud. I could not possibly square the circle as requested, and ended up keeping almost everything, filed and sorted.

Be patient, little mermaid. Some day your place in the zeitgeist may come ...

1 In quoting from Saville's notes, I have retained the inconsistent orthography of the original.

2 One of the more melancholy *Prisoner* slogans, 'Be seeing you', was an earlier Saville suggestion for the present book's title.

Archive 2002
Photography Nathan Gale
Image manipulation Tom Skipp

190

Photographic acknowledgements

All Trevor Key images courtesy of the estate of
Trevor Key.
My Life in the Bush of Ghosts © Brian Eno.
Wham! artwork and logo with kind permission of
George Michael and Sony Music.
Revenge courtesy of Suze Randall, www.suze.net
Yves Klein's *Untitled blue monochrome* (IKB 175)
© ADAGP, Paris.
Kevin Cummins photograph reproduced with
kind permission of Idols.
Dynamo and journal cover by Fortunato Depero
courtesy of the Casa Museo Depero di Rovereto.
Giorgio de Chirico's *The Evil Genius of a King*
courtesy of Gaia Bianchi di Lavagne and Valentina
Bandelloni at SCALA Picture Library.
Josef Muller-Brockmann's *Der Film* poster
courtesy of Shizuko Yoshikawa and © DACS.
Funkapolitan reproduced with kind permission
of Tom Dixon.
After 'After Monarch of the Glen' is published by
Paul Stolper.

Thanks to Alan Parks at London Records, Rebecca
Boulton at Prime Management, Ray Bird at Virgin
Records, Julie Brown at MAP, Emma Greenhalgh
and Nathalie Ours at Yohji Yamamoto.

Contributors

Peter Hall is a contributing writer for *Metropolis* magazine in New York and senior editor at the Design Institute, University of Minnesota. He also teaches at Yale School of Art's MFA graphic design program. Recent writings include the book *Sagmeister: Made you Look* and an upcoming essay on the history of the elevator interior.

Emily King is design editor of *frieze* magazine. Her book *Restart: New Systems in Graphic Design* was published by Thames and Hudson in 2001 and in 2002 she curated two graphic design exhibitions: *Design Now: Graphics* for the Design Museum, London and *The Book Corner* for the British Council.

Over the years **Paul Morley** has worked in various capacities with the BBC, Brian Eno, *NME*, Channel 4, New Order, *The Guardian*, Reeves and Mortimer, Faber and Faber, Art of Noise, *Esquire*, Grace Jones, Anton Corbijn. He has just written a book for Bloomsbury about the history of popular music from the big bang to around about now.

Rick Poynor's books about design and visual culture include two essay collections, *Design without Boundaries* (1998) and *Obey the Giant: Life in the Image World* (2001). *No More Rules*, a critical study of graphic design and postmodernism, will be published in autumn 2003.

Journalist **Miranda Sawyer** lives in Brixton, but grew up in and around Manchester. The Haçienda provided several of her formative experiences, including a fashion show hosted by Frank Sidebottom, gigs by Felt and A Certain Ratio and several unreportable events in the Gay Traitor bar.

Christopher Wilson is a freelance designer and writer. Design clients include Booth-Clibborn Editions, Laurence King Publishing, London Arts (with Phil Baines) and Tate Liverpool (with Richard Hollis). His writing has appeared in *DotDotDot*, *Eye*, *Graphics International* and *TypoGraphic*.

Peter Wallis was co-founder of the influential management consultancy SRU with Lord Stevenson (now Chairman of Pearson PLC, Halifax PLC and The Appointments Commission). He is also well known as **Peter York**, the writer, author and broadcaster on social styles and trends. He is a columnist for the *Independent on Sunday, Management Today* and *GQ*.

Do you think design is …
No.

What?
No.

Do you think design is …
No. No, I don't.